# The make-ahead Kitchen

## To my children

May you always love good food, appreciate healthy
home-cooking, and enjoy the little things in life.
And, of course, may you always find
love and JOY in the kitchen!

# The make-ahead Kitchen

## annalise thomas

75 Slow-Cooker, Freezer, and Prepared Meals for the Busy Lifestyle

FRONT TABLE BOOKS | AN IMPRINT OF CEDAR FORT, INC. | SPRINGVILLE, UTAH

ISBN 13: 978-1-4621-1726-0

Published by Front Table Books, an imprint of Cedar Fort, Inc.
2373 W. 700 S., Springville, UT 84663
Distributed by Cedar Fort, Inc., www.cedarfort.com

LIBRARY OF CONGRESS CATALOGING-IN-PUBLICATION DATA

Names: Thomas, Annalise, 1981- author.
Title: Make-Ahead Kitchen / Annalise Thomas.
Description: Springville, Utah : Front Table Books, 2016. | Includes index.
Identifiers: LCCN 2015036608 | ISBN 9781462117260 (layflat binding : acid-free paper)
Subjects: LCSH: Cooking. | LCGFT: Cookbooks.
Classification: LCC TX714 .T4934 2016 | DDC 641.5--dc23
LC record available at http://lccn.loc.gov/2015036608

Cover and page design by M. Shaun McMurdie
Cover design © 2016 by Cedar Fort, Inc.
Edited by Justin Greer

Printed in the United States of America

10  9  8  7  6  5  4  3  2

Printed on acid-free paper

# contents

# acknowledgments

I want to thank my family for your patience in the craziness of cooking/baking/photographing/writing this book, and my friends, extended family, and blog readers for your willing tastebuds, honest critiques, and endless encouragement.

Your love and support has made me who I am today, and this journey wouldn't have happened without each one of you. Thank you for being on this wild ride with me and being such a big part of making my dreams come true!

# general notes

I use the scoop-and-sweep method for measuring flour in all of my recipes. Dip your measuring cup into your flour to gently overfill the cup and then sweep across the top with a straight edge (a butter knife or spatula handle works well for this!). But here's a note on that, that will apply to some of you. If you don't go through your flour very quickly in general, you will need to 'fluff' your flour. The easiest way to do this is to stick a clean whisk in the container and stir a few times. That will keep the flour from being so heavy it alters the results of your baking! (And that is also why European cookbooks use weight measurements. It's much more accurate!)

Whenever a recipe calls for butter, I am referring to salted butter. I am one of the old-school team who likes salted butter best. I have yet to ever come across a recipe that turned out 'too salty' because of using salted butter! Maybe someday I will convert to the unsalted team, but for now I am all about that salt.

Recipe yields: Please don't hate me on this one . . . but you know I just can't promise that a recipe will make exactly 47.5 cookies, right? I have no idea how many 'tastes' you will need to take of that delicious cookie dough, or exactly how big your scoop is. So, take my yields as a general idea and go from there. If you need 100 of the Hawaiian Oatmeal Sandwich Cookies, you're gonna need to make a few batches and count what you have, k? We like cookie dough in this house. I can never seem to keep all of our fingers out of the bowl long enough to get an accurate cookie count!

Check your oven temperature. Or watch whatever you're cooking or baking closely as it gets close to the end. Some ovens run as much as 25 degrees hotter than others! Keep an eye on yours and you will get a feel for how to adjust recipes. Always go by the 'doneness' indicators of a recipe more than the time. Shorter or longer is fine, as long as the end result turns out the way you want!

This is by no means a gluten-free cookbook, but you will find several recipes with gluten-free variations on them. Not everyone struggles with gluten allergies or sensitivities, but I'm sure we all at least know someone who does. I love to have a stash of tried-and-true gluten-free recipes in my pocket so that I can spoil the people I love that have sensitivities too. My gluten-free recipes are all tested to be great for everyone. Even those with no sensitivities will love these goodies (and often not even realize they're different!). Also, you will find a symbol (gluten-free = GF; gluten-free alternative = GFA) on all recipes that are naturally GF, so you know right away!

# introduction

Life is crazy. It is full of busy, and there are so many things that can add stress to your days. Cooking should not be one of them; sharing food should bring you together. Often we are rushed into grabbing the first thing we can find, or giving in to expensive ready-made foods when our families are hungry, and we lose out on the joy of really savoring our food.

This is where a make-ahead cooking lifestyle comes in. With a little bit of thought and planning, delicious home-cooked meals can be ready for you to enjoy when you and your family need them. All it takes is a few minutes here and there (when you have time!) and some room in your fridge and freezer.

Not all of the dishes in this book are freezer meals. Some are, but others are just as simple as a wonderful salad you can prep a few days in advance or delicious steel-cut oatmeal you can throw into the slow cooker before bed, waking up to the most amazing aroma and breakfast ready for you in the morning.

However you like to spend your time in the kitchen, I promise that you can make your food-life a little easier and a lot more fun with even just a few of the recipes in this book. My dream is that each one of you will learn to love cooking wholesome, made-from-scratch meals for you and your loved ones to enjoy.

Thank you for letting me join you in your kitchen. I'm so happy to be here!

# breakfasts

# maple bacon overnight cinnamon rolls

*As if you needed more reason to make these cinnamon rolls than the name alone. Maple. Bacon. Overnight Cinnamon Rolls. Enough said!*

**FOR THE DOUGH:**

2 cups evaporated milk

½ cup butter

⅓ cup sugar

2¼ teaspoons active dry yeast

4½ cups flour, divided

½ teaspoon baking powder

½ teaspoon baking soda

1 teaspoon salt

**FOR THE FILLING:**

½ cup butter

½ cup firmly packed brown sugar

½ cup sugar

1 tablespoon cinnamon

**FOR THE FROSTING:**

4 cups powdered sugar

2 tablespoons melted butter

2 tablespoons milk

2 tablespoons strong brewed coffee

1 tablespoon maple flavoring

½ pound bacon, cooked and crumbled

**1**  In a large dutch oven, heat the milk, butter, and sugar together over medium heat until the butter is melted and the milk is steaming and just starting to form little bubbles around the edges. Move the pot off the heat and let cool to room temperature, stirring occasionally.

**2**  When the milk mixture has cooled down to just barely warm (after an hour or so), stir in the yeast and 4 cups of the flour until just combined. Cover with a clean towel, move the pot back onto a burner, turn the heat on LOW for 2–3 minutes, and then turn off

and let rest for an hour. In a small bowl, stir together the remaining ½ cup flour and the baking powder, baking soda, and salt. Set aside.

**3**  The dough will be puffy and almost doubled in size after an hour. Stir in the remaining flour mixture until just well combined. Place the pot of dough, covered, into the fridge for an hour or two, if you have time, to make the dough a bit easier to handle. Otherwise, just continue on!

**4**  When you are ready to start assembling the rolls, take the dough out of the fridge. (If it has been in there for longer than an hour or two, and it's too cold to work with, let it rest at room temperature for a bit until it softens enough to roll out.)

**5**  Roll out the dough into a very large rectangle (about ¼" thick all over—size doesn't matter as much as even thickness!). Spread the butter evenly (you can your hands!) all over the top of the dough, leaving about ¼-inch border at the top edge. Mix the sugars and cinnamon together in a small bowl and then sprinkle evenly all over the buttered dough. Press down gently.

**6**  Starting at the long end (closest to you), roll the dough up into a log, pinching the ends gently to keep the filling inside and resting the roll seam-side down. With a sharp serrated knife, cut the roll into 15 individual rolls and place them cut sides up into a buttered 9×13" baking dish. Cover with plastic wrap and place in the fridge overnight.

**7**  In the morning, remove the pan from the fridge, place it on the counter, and let it rest while you preheat the oven to 375°F for half an hour or so.

**8**  Remove the plastic and bake for 15–20 minutes, until the rolls are golden brown. (If your pans are glass, check the bottoms to see if they are golden too. Or take a butter knife and peek into one of the center rolls to make sure the dough is cooked all the way through!).

**9**  While the cinnamon rolls are baking, whip up the frosting. In a large bowl, whisk together the powdered sugar, butter, milk, coffee, and maple flavoring until smooth. If it's too thin, add more powdered sugar a bit at a time, and if it's too thick, add a bit more liquid. You really can't go wrong with frosting!

**10**  When the cinnamon rolls come out of the oven, spread them with as much frosting as you'd like and top with the crumbled bacon!

*Serves 12–15*

# roasted veggie & ham overnight egg bake 🍃GF

*This is not your usual carb-loaded egg bake full of bread or potatoes.*

*This is a flavorful, rich, but low-carb egg bake that is incredibly delicious, packed full of flavor, and ready before you go to bed.*

*All you have to do in the morning is preheat the oven and pop the dish in to bake! Serve with some fresh fruit & lots of hot coffee for weekend brunch perfection!*

1 large onion, chopped

2 large bell peppers, chopped (2 different colors!)

1 jalapeño, seeded and chopped

½ pound sliced fresh mushrooms, optional

2 cups diced ham

1 bunch green onions, sliced thinly

1 cup shredded pepperjack or mozzarella cheese

1 cup shredded cheddar cheese

12 large eggs

½ cup half & half

½ teaspoon salt

½ teaspoon pepper

paprika or cayenne pepper

**1**   Preheat the oven to 450°F. Grease a 9×13" baking dish. Set aside.

**2**   Toss the onions, all the peppers, and the mushrooms (if using) in a small drizzle of melted coconut oil or olive oil—and some salt and pepper—and roast for 25–40 minutes (time will depend on how big your veggies are chopped!) until golden. Watch carefully at the end so they don't burn! Transfer the veggies (and don't forget to scrape up the yummy bits on the pan!) into the greased baking dish and let cool completely.

**3**   When the roasted veggies are cool, layer on the ham, green onions, and shredded cheeses.

**4**   In a medium bowl, whisk the eggs with the salt and pepper and half & half. Pour this egg mixture over the ingredients in the pan and sprinkle the top with a bit of paprika or cayenne pepper, for color.

**5**   Cover the dish with plastic wrap and place in the fridge to sit overnight.

**6**   In the morning, preheat the oven to 375°F and take the egg bake out of the fridge to wait on the counter. When the oven is hot, remove the plastic and place the dish into the oven to bake for 50–60 minutes, until set and golden on top (peek in the middle with a small knife to make sure the eggs are cooked through!).

**7**   Serve hot, with hot sauce (sriracha is my favorite!) on the side for those who like a little more heat!

Cut any leftovers into squares and place in airtight containers. Place in the fridge or freezer and reheat for a quick, easy breakfast another day!

*Serves 10–12*

# peach pecan coconut breakfast bars

*There is no better way to enjoy summer stone fruit season than peaches in every form. I know it's hard to keep from just eating their juicy goodness right out of hand, but if you can set a few aside, make these delicious breakfast bars.*

*They are perfect for a weekend brunch or an afternoon treat with coffee. Sweet, but not too sweet, you can kick them up to dessert land with a bit of vanilla ice cream or enjoy them in breakfast/brunch just the way they are!*

**FOR THE CRUST:**

2 cups flour

½ cup firmly packed brown sugar

½ cup cold butter, diced

4–6 tablespoons very cold water

**FOR THE FILLING:**

4 large eggs

2 cups firmly packed brown sugar

2 teaspoons pure almond extract

½ cup flour

1 teaspoon baking powder

½ teaspoon salt

2 cups flaked, sweetened coconut

1 cup chopped pecans

4 large, ripe peaches, peeled and diced

**1**  Preheat the oven to 350°F. Grease a 9×13" baking dish. Set aside.

**2**  In a large bowl, mix together the 2 cups flour and ½ cup brown sugar. Cut in the butter with cold fingers or a pastry blender, until the mixture resembles coarse meal. Sprinkle 2 tablespoons of water over the top and gently toss together with your fingers or a fork. Sprinkle on 2 more tablespoons and toss gently again. Test the dough by grabbing a small handful and pressing it together. If it comes together, you are done. If not, keep adding water a tablespoon at a time, until the dough just comes together. Press into the 9×13" baking dish and bake for 15 minutes, until just set.

**3**  In a large mixing bowl, beat the eggs until smooth. Beat in the brown sugar, a little at a time, until smooth again, and then stir in the almond extract. In a small bowl, whisk together the ½ cup flour, baking powder and salt. Stir this into the egg and sugar mixture and blend well. Remove from the mixer and gently fold in the coconut, pecans, and peaches with a spatula.

**4**  Take the crust out of the oven and pour the peach mixture over the warm crust. Return to the oven to bake for another 45–60 minutes, until lightly golden on the top and just set. Let cool completely before cutting and serving, dusted with powdered sugar or topped with fresh whipped cream if you'd like!

You can make these bars ahead, cool them completely, and freeze in an airtight container for up to 3 months. Thaw on the counter for a few hours or in the fridge overnight and serve!

*Serves 15–20*

# pumpkin pie slow cooker oatmeal ⬱GF

*If you've never experienced slow cooker oatmeal, you are in for a treat. I can't even tell you how amazing it is to wake up to the smell of this oatmeal. Add in a programmable coffee maker, and you've got hands-free morning bliss right there!*

*Throw this easy breakfast together in 2 minutes before you go to bed, turn the slow cooker on LOW and go to sleep. You will wake up to a delicious, hearty breakfast the whole family will love!*

*But be warned . . . you may just find yourself wanting to top this breakfast with a mound of fresh whipped cream and some toasted pecans!*

4 cups water

½ cup milk (or almond milk)

2 cups old-fashioned rolled oats

1 cup pumpkin purée

½–1 cup firmly packed brown sugar (to taste)

2 tablespoons butter or coconut oil

1 tablespoon pumpkin pie spice

1 tablespoon cinnamon

½ teaspoon salt

**1**  Stir all of the ingredients together in the slow cooker. Cook on LOW* overnight, at least 8 hours. (If you think your slow cooker runs hot, cook this on KEEP WARM overnight to keep it from burning!)

**2**  When it is done, give it a good stir so everything comes together and serve with your favorite oatmeal toppings!

You can store any leftover oatmeal in individual containers in the fridge to reheat for super quick breakfasts later in the week, or scoop into greased muffin tins, freeze, and then pop out into a freezer bag for even longer storage!

*Serves 5–6*

*Everyone has a family banana bread recipe in their pocket, but if you've never tried a sour-cream version, you are definitely missing out! This bread is so moist it really doesn't even need to be served with butter . . . but I will say that has never stopped me!*

3 cups all-purpose flour

2 teaspoons cinnamon

2 teaspoons salt

2 teaspoons baking soda

1 cup butter, softened

2 cups sugar

4 large eggs

1 tablespoon pure vanilla extract

2 cups mashed very ripe bananas (about 4 large or 6 medium bananas)

1 cup sour cream

**1**  Preheat the oven to 350°F. Butter two 9×5" loaf pans. Set aside.

**2**  In a medium bowl, stir together the flour, cinnamon, salt, and baking soda until combined. Set aside.

**3**  In a large mixing bowl, cream together the butter and sugar until light and fluffy. Beat in the eggs, one at a time, and the vanilla.

**4**  Add in ⅓ of the flour mixture and stir on low until just combined. Then stir in the mashed bananas until just combined. Add another ⅓ of the flour mixture, stir, and then the sour cream and the remaining flour. Stir until just well combined, being careful not to over-mix.

**5**  Spread the batter into the loaf pans and bake for 50–60 minutes, until a toothpick inserted in the center of a loaf comes out with just a few crumbs. Let cool for 10 minutes in the pans and gently turn out onto cooling racks to cool completely.

These loaves freeze beautifully. Cool completely, wrap well in plastic wrap, and place in freezer bags. Freeze for up to 3 months. Thaw on the counter overnight before serving.

*Makes two 9x5" loaves*

# extra-moist freezer-friendly cinnamon banana bread

# big batch maple-glazed make-ahead cinnamon rolls

*Okay, okay. I know this is a HUGE amount of cinnamon rolls. But before you run away screaming, let me tell you my thoughts.*

*You may recognize the method of these cinnamon rolls from The Pioneer Woman Ree Drummond's famous cinnamon rolls. I love her no-fuss, no-knead method, and, with lots of tweaks, I used to make a small batch of them for my family.*

*One day, I just woke up and realized I had been wasting my time! It really is hardly any more work to make this whole huge batch, and since you're already making a mess and cinnamon rolls freeze so beautifully—and share so beautifully—and make so many people happy—you'd really have to reach far to convince me that you can't make this!*

*Do you have friends? Do you have family? Do you have a freezer? Do you have coworkers? Do you have neighbors? If you answered yes to any of those questions, you have a reason to make this big ol' batch.*

*You will make so many people, or your freezer, very happy. And if you're going to make the mess of cinnamon rolls (because let's face it, it's a bit of a messy job!), you might as well go all out and get your effort's worth!*

3⅓ cups lowfat milk

⅔ cup heavy cream

1 cup butter

¾ cup sugar

4½ teaspoons (or two packets) active dry yeast

9 cups flour, divided (8 cups + 1 cup)

1 teaspoon baking powder

1 teaspoon baking soda

2 teaspoons salt

1½ cups butter, softened

1 cup sugar

1 cup firmly packed brown sugar

3 tablespoons ground cinnamon

1 teaspoon ground nutmeg

5 cups powdered sugar

½ cup softened butter

½ cup (or so) milk

1 tablespoon maple flavoring

¼ teaspoon salt

**1**   In a large (6 quart or bigger) dutch oven, heat the milk, cream, butter, and sugar together over medium heat until the butter, is melted and the milk is steaming and just starting to form little bubbles around the edges. Move the pot off the heat and let cool to room temperature, stirring occasionally, if you think of it.

**2**   When the milk mixture has cooled down to barely warm (after an hour or two), stir in the yeast and then 8 cups of the flour until just combined. Cover with a clean towel, put the pot back on a burner, turn the heat on LOW for 2–3 minutes, and then turn off and leave alone for an hour. In a small bowl, stir together the remaining 1 cup flour and the baking powder, baking soda, and salt. Set aside.

**3**   The dough will be puffy and almost doubled in size after an hour. Stir in the remaining flour mixture until just well combined. Place the pot of dough, covered, into the fridge for an hour or two.

(You can leave this in the fridge overnight at this point, if you want to continue on tomorrow!)

**4**   When you are ready to start assembling the rolls, take the dough out of the fridge. (If it has been in there for longer than an hour or two, and it's too cold to work with, let it rest at room temperature for a bit until it softens enough to roll out.)

**5**   Butter three 9×13" baking dishes and set aside. In a small bowl, stir together the sugar, brown sugar, cinnamon, and nutmeg; set aside.

**6**   Divide the dough into 3 parts and remove one part at a time from the pot and roll out into a large rectangle on a floured surface. With your hands (yes, your hands), gently rub ½ cup of softened butter onto the rolled out dough, covering the surface evenly. Sprinkle ⅓ of the sugar–cinnamon mixture evenly over the top of the butter.

**7** Starting at the long end, roll the dough up into a log, pinching the ends gently to keep the filling inside and resting the roll seam-side down. With a sharp serrated knife, cut the roll into 12 individual rolls and place them cut sides up into one of the buttered baking dishes. Cover lightly with plastic wrap and repeat the rolling and filling process with the other two batches of dough.

**8** Once all of the rolls are in their pans covered with plastic wrap, turn on the oven to preheat to 375°F. Let the rolls rise on the counter while the oven preheats and then remove the plastic and bake for 15–20 minutes, until the rolls are golden brown. (If your pans are glass, check the bottoms to see if they are golden too. Or take a butter knife and peek into one of the center rolls to make sure the dough is cooked all the way through!).

**9** While the rolls are baking, whip up some frosting to go on top. You can use any cinnamon roll frosting you like. My favorite is this simple maple powdered sugar glaze. (My family is divided on our opinions of what cinnamon roll frosting should look like. I like a drizzle, some of the kids prefer naked rolls, and my husband likes his drowned in any form of sugary frosting. Whatever floats your boat!)

In a medium bowl, whisk together the powdered sugar, butter, maple extract, salt, and milk until smooth. Set aside until the rolls come out of the oven.

**10** While the pans of cinnamon rolls are still hot, pour the frosting over each pan, covering the rolls completely. (If you don't like much frosting, make a thinner glaze with more milk so the rolls are still covered completely. This keeps them fresher longer!)

**11** Cool completely before eating, or wrapping well and freezing for up to several weeks!

*Wrap the baked, frosted, and cooled cinnamon rolls well in plastic wrap, foil, and even into gallon ziploc freezer bags if you are using the small round disposable pans and freeze for up to 3 months. Let them thaw on the counter overnight before serving. And you can warm them up in a low oven for a few minutes if you'd like!*

If you are just serving these the next day, they can be covered well and left out at room temperature. The maple glaze will keep them tasting fresh as can be even the next day!

*Makes 36 rolls in three 9x13" pans or 6 disposable round pans*

# coconut spice zucchini bread

*Do you have an abundance of zucchini in your garden? Or a neighbor with too much zucchini who keeps offering to send some your way?*

*Well, now your problems are solved! This zucchini bread is above and beyond. Moist, flavorful, packed with coconut, and a tiny bit healthier than most recipes. Give it a try next time you are overwhelmed with zucchini. You won't regret it!*

3 cups flour

1 teaspoon baking soda

1 teaspoon baking powder

1 teaspoon salt

2 teaspoons ground cinnamon

½ teaspoon ground nutmeg

½ teaspoon ground ginger

3 cups shredded fresh or frozen zucchini (skin on)

¾ cup firmly packed brown sugar

¾ cup sugar

½ cup melted coconut oil or butter

1 cup sour cream

2 large eggs

2 teaspoons pure vanilla extract

2 cups shredded, UNsweetened coconut

**1**   With clean hands, wring out the shredded zucchini well over a large colander in the sink until most of the liquid is squeezed out. If you are using frozen shredded zucchini, let it thaw in a colander, and then squeeze out any excess.

**2**   In a large bowl, whisk together the flour, baking soda, baking powder, salt, cinnamon, nutmeg, and ginger. Set aside.

**3**   In another large bowl, whisk together the sugars, coconut oil, sour cream, eggs, & vanilla until well blended. Pour the wet ingredients into the bowl with the dry ingredients and stir gently to combine.

**4**   Stir in the shredded coconut and zucchini and divide evenly into the 2 prepared loaf pans. Bake for 50–60 minutes, until a toothpick inserted in the center comes out almost clean (a few crumbs is good—wet batter is not!).

**5**   Let cool before slicing and serving.

Wrap the completely cooled loaves well in plastic wrap and foil and place in freezer bags for up to 3 months! Thaw overnight on the counter.

*Makes two 9x5" loaves*

# easy cardamom sweet cream biscuits

*Of course you can leave the cardamom out of these biscuits or substitute with cinnamon for a fun twist, but if you've never used cardamom before, give it a try!*

*I like to serve these with butter and homemade strawberry freezer jam for breakfast, or turn them into dessert with my roasted strawberry-rhubarb sauce and a bit of fresh whipped cream!*

4 cups flour

¼ cup sugar

2 tablespoons baking powder

1 tablespoon ground cardamom

1 teaspoon salt

2½ cups heavy cream (plus a bit more if needed)

melted butter to brush the tops

**1**  Preheat the oven to 425°F. Line 2 baking sheets with parchment and set aside.

**2**  In a large bowl, whisk together the flour, sugar, baking powder, cardamom, and salt. Pour the 2½ cups heavy cream over the top and gently stir and fold with a spatula. Be very gentle with this and keep folding until the mixture starts to feel moist and comes together in your hands. If it is too dry and crumbly, add a bit more cream a tablespoon at a time, until it comes together when pressed in a ball in your hand.

**3**  Gently dump the dough out onto a floured board and press into a square about ¾"–1" thick. Cut into 16 pieces and place 8 squares on each baking sheet. Brush the tops with a little bit of melted butter.

**4**  Place a baking sheet into the preheated oven and bake for 12–15 minutes, until the tops are lightly golden brown. Let cool and serve!

At this point, you can bake them both, or you can stick one pan into the freezer for another time. As soon as the unbaked biscuits are completely frozen, transfer them to a plastic freezer bag and store up to 3 months. When you are ready to bake them, pull them straight out of the freezer and just add a few more minutes to the baking time!

*Serves 12–16*

# coconut brown sugar cinnamon rolls

*It doesn't take more than a tiny drizzle of glaze on these babies (or none at all!), and they are so much more fun than a plain old cinnamon roll!*

*If you like coconut at all, you will love this fun twist on the usual!*

**FOR THE DOUGH:**

2 cups evaporated milk

1 tablespoon sugar

⅓ cup butter

2¼ teaspoons (or one packet) active dry yeast

4½ cups flour, divided (4 cups + ½ cup)

½ teaspoon baking powder

½ teaspoon baking soda

1 teaspoon salt

**FOR THE FILLING:**

½ cup butter, very soft

⅓ firmly packed brown sugar

1 tablespoon cinnamon

2 cups sweetened flaked coconut

**FOR THE GLAZE:**

1 cup powdered sugar

2 tablespoons milk

1 tablespoons butter, very soft

1 teaspoon maple flavoring

**1**   In a large dutch oven, heat the milk, sugar, and butter together over medium heat until the butter is melted and the milk is steaming and just starting to form little bubbles around the edges. Move the pot off the heat and let cool to room temperature, stirring occasionally.

**2**   When the milk mixture has cooled down to barely warm (after an hour or so), stir in the yeast and 4 cups of the flour until just combined. Cover with a clean towel, put the pot back on a burner, turn the heat on LOW for 2–3 minutes, and then turn off and leave alone for an hour. In a small bowl, stir together the remaining ½ cup flour and the baking powder, baking soda, and salt. Set aside.

**3**   The dough will be puffy and almost doubled in size after an hour. Stir in the remaining flour mixture until just well combined. Place the pot of dough, covered, into the fridge for an hour or two.

(You can leave this in the fridge overnight at this point, if you want to continue on tomorrow!)

**4**   When you are ready to start assembling the rolls, take the dough out of the fridge. (If it has been in there for longer than an hour or two, and it's too cold to work with, let it rest at room temperature for a bit until it softens enough to roll out.)

**5**   Roll out the dough into a very large rectangle (about ¼-inch thick all over—size doesn't matter as much as even thickness!). Spread the butter evenly (use your hands!) all over the top of the dough, leaving about ¼-inch border at the top edge. Mix the brown sugar and cinnamon together in a small bowl, and then sprinkle evenly all over the buttered dough. Sprinkle 2 cups of sweetened flaked coconut all over the sugar and press down gently.

**6**   Starting at the long end (closest to you), roll the dough up into a log, pinch the ends gently to keep the filling inside, and rest the roll seam-side down. With a sharp serrated knife, cut the roll into 15 individual rolls and place them cut sides up into a buttered 9×13" baking dish. Cover lightly with plastic wrap and let rise while you preheat the oven to 375°F for a half hour or so.

**7**   Remove the plastic and bake for 15–20 minutes, until the rolls are golden brown. (If your pans are glass, check the bottoms to see if they are golden too. Or take a butter knife and peek into one of the center rolls to make sure the dough is cooked all the way through!)

**8**   If you'd like, whip up a simple powdered sugar glaze to drizzle on top for looks. (This is totally optional, of course, but what fun is a cinnamon roll without at least a little drizzle!) Whisk together the powdered sugar, milk, butter, and flavoring until very smooth. Add a bit more milk if it's too thick, or a bit more powdered sugar if it's too thin. Drizzle over the warm rolls and let them cool before serving!

These cinnamon rolls freeze beautifully. Let them cool completely, wrap well in plastic wrap and foil, and freeze. Pull them out and let them thaw overnight on the counter before serving. You can warm them up for a few minutes in the oven once they've thawed, if you'd like!

*Serves 12–15*

# double dark chocolate banana bread

*There is nothing boring about this banana bread. Moist, rich, chocolatey, and full of flavor, it will impress anyone you serve it to.*

*Do you have a chocolate lover in your life? Make them some of this banana bread. You might just get a proposal. Or a new best friend!*

2 heaping cups mashed very ripe bananas

1 cup organic virgin coconut oil, melted

1½ cups firmly packed brown sugar

2 large eggs

2 teaspoons pure vanilla extract

1 teaspoon pure almond extract

2 cups flour

1 cup dutch processed cocoa powder

2 teaspoons baking soda

1½ teaspoons salt

½ cup mini-chocolate chips

**1**  Preheat the oven to 350°F. Grease two 9×5" loaf pans with baking spray.

**2**  In a large bowl, whisk together the bananas, melted coconut oil, brown sugar, eggs, and extracts until they are well mixed.

**3**  In a medium bowl, whisk together the flour, cocoa powder, baking soda, and salt. Gently stir this flour mixture into the bowl with the banana mixture until just combined. Divide the batter evenly into the two greased loaf pans.

**4**  Sprinkle ¼ cup of the mini chocolate chips onto the top of each pan and bake for 50–60 minutes, until a toothpick inserted in the center comes out almost clean (a few crumbs is fine!).

**5**  Let cool for 10–15 minutes in the pan, and then transfer to a cooling rack to cool completely before slicing.

To freeze, let cool completely, wrap each loaf well in plastic wrap, and place in a large freezer bag. Freeze for up to 3 months! To serve, thaw on the counter overnight.

*Makes two 9x5" loaves*

# sour cream pumpkin bread

*So many quick breads, so little time. My fall-loving soul is in love with this one. Pumpkin everything is my love language, and this one is no exception.*

*So moist, so cozy, so perfectly fall. Bake up a few loaves and store some in your freezer. You will be so happy to have this in supply!*

3½ cups flour

1 tablespoon pumpkin pie spice

1 tablespoon cinnamon

2 teaspoons baking soda

2 teaspoons salt

½ cup butter, melted and slightly cooled

½ cup sour cream

1½ cups sugar

1½ cups firmly packed brown sugar

4 large eggs

⅔ cup milk

2 cups pumpkin purée

2 teaspoons pure vanilla extract

**1**   Preheat the oven to 350°F. Grease two 9" loaf pans. Set aside.

**2**   In a medium bowl, whisk together the flour, pumpkin pie spice, cinnamon, baking soda, and salt; Set aside.

**3**   In a large mixing bowl, mix together the rest of the ingredients until smooth. Mix in the flour slowly until just combined. Spread evenly into two 9" loaf pans and bake for 55–65 minutes, until a toothpick inserted in the center comes out almost clean.

This quick bread freezes beautifully, of course. Wrap well and place in freezer bags. Freeze for up to 3 months. Thaw overnight on the counter and serve with butter or your spread of choice!

*Makes two 9x5" loaf pans*

# overnight, baked maple pecan french toast

*There's nothing better than knowing that your breakfast the next morning is almost done for you. This french toast is special enough to serve for company or Christmas morning, but also easy enough to make anytime you feel like it.*

*Golden french toast with a glorious caramel pecan topping that almost makes this feel like dessert. But don't worry—it's still breakfast!*

3 large eggs, lightly beaten

1 cup milk

¾ cup heavy cream

1 teaspoon pure vanilla extract

1 teaspoon cinnamon

1 (1-pound) loaf french bread, sliced thick

½ cup butter, melted

1 cup firmly packed brown sugar

¼ cup pure maple syrup

1 cup chopped pecans

1 teaspoon cinnamon

**1**  Butter a 9×13" baking dish. Set aside.

**2**  In a medium bowl, whisk together the eggs, milk, cream, vanilla, and 1 teaspoon cinnamon. Dip the bread slices into the mixture and pressing down gently, flipping, and pressing down gently again to coat well. Place them into the buttered baking dish, overlapping them slightly if needed. Cover with plastic wrap and place in the fridge overnight.

**3**  In a small bowl, whisk together the melted butter, brown sugar, maple syrup, and pecans. Cover and leave on the counter overnight (or you can do this in the morning!).

**4**  In the morning, take the french toast out of the fridge and preheat the oven to 350°F. Spoon the caramel pecan mixture over the top of the french toast and bake for 40–45 minutes, until golden. Serve warm, with more maple syrup on the side, if desired!

*Serves 6~8*

# maple nut granola   🌿GF

*Granola is granola is granola, right? It's easy to make, easy to buy, easy to eat. But if you're still buying your granola at the store, I'm asking you right now to stop it. It's just too easy to make it yourself, exactly how you like it!*

*Do you like coconut? Great! Love nuts? Add some! Don't like maple? Use honey instead! This is more of a method than an exact recipe. Toss together some oats and your favorite ingredients with some oil and sweetener, and breakfast is served!*

3 cups old-fashioned rolled oats

1 cup chopped nuts (pecans, sliced almonds, walnuts, or your favorite)

1 cup shredded or flaked coconut

¼ cup melted coconut oil

¼ cup pure maple syrup

2 tablespoons water

1 teaspoon maple flavoring, optional

½ teaspoon salt

**1**  Preheat the oven to 250°F. Toss together the oats, nuts, and coconut on a large, rimmed baking sheet. Mix the rest of the ingredients together in a small bowl and pour over the oat mixture, tossing well to coat.

**2**  Bake for 45–60 minutes, until golden and toasty, stirring once. Let cool completely and transfer to an airtight container. Store at room temperature for up to 2 weeks!

*Serves 8–10*

# blueberry cardamom sour cream coffee cake

*There is no shortage of blueberries in this coffee cake. And I don't say that lightly. This is not an "I wish there were more blueberries in here" treat; it's more of an "I can't believe this many berries are going in this recipe"!*

*Well, believe it. And enjoy it. If you've ever eaten a blueberry muffin wishing there were more blueberries than what you got, this is the recipe for you!*

**FOR THE CAKE:**

½ cup butter, softened

1 cup sugar

2 large eggs

2 cups flour

1 teaspoon baking powder

1 teaspoon baking soda

1 teaspoon ground cardamom

½ teaspoon salt

1 cup sour cream

3 cups blueberries, fresh or frozen (do not thaw if frozen)

**FOR THE TOPPING:**

½ cup firmly packed brown sugar

½ cup flour

½ teaspoon ground cinnamon

½ teaspoon ground nutmeg

½ teaspoon ground cardamom

¼ cup butter, softened

**1**   Preheat the oven to 375°F. Grease a 9×9" square baking dish and set aside.

**2**   In a large mixing bowl, cream together the butter and sugar until light and fluffy, about 3–5 minutes. Beat in the eggs one at a time until blended. In a separate bowl, whisk together the flour, baking powder, baking soda, cardamom, and salt.

**3**   Dump ⅓ of the flour mixture into the mixer and beat on low until just combined. Beat in half of the sour cream. Repeat with another ⅓ of the flour mixture, the sour cream, and the last of the flour. With a spatula, gently fold in the blueberries. Try not to mush them too much!

**4**   Spread the batter into the greased baking dish.

**5**   In a medium bowl, mix together the topping ingredients until the butter is all mixed in and clumps when you squeeze a bit. Sprinkle this on top of the batter and press down lightly.

**6**   Bake for 45–55 minutes, or until the coffee cake is golden on the top and a toothpick inserted in the center comes out with no wet batter.

This recipe can also be doubled if you have a big enough deep 9×13" casserole dish to feed a crowd—adjust baking time, of course! And you may want to triple the topping, if that's your thing!

*Serves 8~9*

# coconut black bottom muffins

*Is it a muffin, or is it a cupcake? That's all up to you, but I choose to camp on the muffin side of the debate, because there's no frosting on these sweet little things—and, obviously, if I call it a muffin I get to serve it for breakfast!*

*Whatever you call it, if you like coconut and black-bottom 'whatever's, this is the recipe you have been looking for!*

### FOR THE FILLING:

1 (8-ounce) brick cream cheese, softened

⅓ cup sugar

1 large egg, room temperature

½ cup sweetened flaked coconut

1 cup mini chocolate chips

### FOR THE CUPCAKE BATTER:

1½ cups flour

½ cup firmly packed brown sugar

½ cup sugar

⅓ cup dutch processed unsweetened cocoa powder

1 teaspoon baking soda

¼ teaspoon salt

1 cup coffee (room temperature)

⅓ cup coconut oil

1 tablespoon apple cider vinegar

1 teaspoon pure vanilla extract

**1   TO MAKE THE FILLING:** In a medium bowl, beat together the cream cheese, ⅓ cup sugar, and egg until smooth. Stir in the coconut and mini chocolate chips, cover, and place in the fridge to chill for at least 2 hours, until firm.

**2   TO MAKE THE CAKE BATTER:** In a large bowl, whisk together the flour, brown sugar, ½ cup sugar, cocoa powder, baking soda, and salt. In a small bowl, whisk together the coffee, coconut oil, apple cider vinegar, and vanilla. Pour the wet ingredients into the dry ingredients and stir gently until just combined.

**3   Preheat the oven to 350°F and line about 48 mini muffin cups with liners, or 24 regular-sized muffin cups. (The number is not exact—you may need a bit more or less, depending on the size of your pans or how full your tins are. Just use what you need!)

**4   Fill each liner ½ full of the chocolate cake batter, and then scoop one tablespoon of the chilled cream cheese mixture and press it down into the center of the cup, until the chocolate just comes up over the sides of the cream cheese.

**5   Bake for 18–25 minutes, depending on the size of your pans—start checking at 18 minutes, and keep checking every few minutes until barely golden on the cream cheese and the cake springs back when pressed lightly.

**6   Let cool completely before serving!

Freeze the cooled muffins in airtight containers for up to 3 months. Thaw overnight on the counter and serve!

*Serves 24~28*

Soups & Salads

# soups & salads

# easy lemony slow cooker chicken noodle soup  ⌇GFA

*I love a good soup. It is one of the easiest meals to throw together in your slow cooker for a quick, effortless meal any time of the year!*

*This recipe has two vital, game-changing ingredients. First is lemon juice. If you have never had lemon in your chicken soup before, you are missing out. It is so bright and fresh and amazing. Add a little, taste, and then add a little more until it is as lemony as you would like. (Or if not everyone is a lemon-lover, serve wedges on the side and squeeze into each bowl as you like!)*

*The next special ingredient is one you may never have used before, but I hope it becomes a second-nature thing. When you buy your big chunk of fresh parmesan cheese to grate (because you do, right? Please tell me you're not still buying that green can. Try the chunk. You will never go back!), save the rinds in a bag in the freezer. Whenever you make soup, or even a meaty pasta sauce, throw in a rind while it's cooking. It melts and saturates your dish with flavor in such an amazing way!*

*One last note: A good chicken soup is only as good as the broth that it starts with. If you make homemade chicken stock, then you are step ahead of the game. Otherwise, buy the best stock you can find. It will make a difference!*

*If you've never made homemade chicken stock, this is the perfect time to try it! Buy a rotisserie chicken, pull of all the meat, and save it for the soup later. Throw all the bones and stuff into a large pot and pour in just enough water to cover. Bring to a boil, reduce the heat to LOW, and simmer for 24–48 hours. Let the broth cool a bit, and then strain into jars and store in the fridge for up to a week (or freezer for up to 3 months!).*

1 large onion, chopped

3 large carrots, chopped

3 large celery stalks, chopped

2 large garlic cloves, finely minced

3 cups cooked, chopped chicken meat

1 chunk parmesan cheese rind

2 bay leaves

½ teaspoon dried oregano

8–12 cups good chicken stock

salt and pepper, to taste

½ pound egg noodles (or GF noodles, if needed), to serve

1–2 large lemons

**1**  Place everything except the noodles and lemon into a large crockpot and stir to combine. Cook on LOW for 8–12 hours, or HIGH for 4–6 hours. When you are almost ready to serve, cook ½ pound egg noodles according to package directions, and then drain and toss them with a bit of butter to keep them from sticking (and to flavor the soup even more!).

**2**  When the soup is ready, squeeze the lemon into a small bowl, fish out the seeds, and then stir the juice into the soup, to taste. Taste for seasoning, adding salt and pepper and more oregano to taste, if you'd like. Find the parmesan rind and bay leaves and pull them out of the soup.

**3**  To serve, place a generous scoop of noodles into each bowl and then ladle the bowl full of soup. Serve immediately and feel the comfort coursing through your veins with each bite!

Store any leftover soup with the noodles kept separate to keep them from dissolving into mush in your soup!

This soup freezes beautifully for up to 3 months—without the noodles, of course. You could even freeze all of the ingredients except the noodles, lemon, and chicken stock in a large freezer bag and then just stir in the stock and continue the recipe when you are ready to make it!

*Serves 8–10*

# thick & hearty split pea & ham soup ⬤GF

*There is nothing I love better on a cold winter's day than a big bowl of steaming hot split pea soup, with a side of crusty french bread.*

*It really is the best comfort food. And if you think you don't like split pea soup, please don't write this recipe off before you try it. I have served this to many self-proclaimed "split-pea-soup-haters," and every single one of them has told me that they love this soup!*

*So give it a try! It doesn't get much easier than a big pot of soup that will feed you for days, and only gets better as it sits!*

2 tablespoons bacon grease, coconut oil, or olive oil

1 large onion, chopped

2 large carrots, chopped

3 large celery stalks, chopped

2 large garlic cloves, minced

1 large smoked ham hock (or the meaty bone leftover from bone-in ham!)

6–8 cups chicken stock (plus water as needed to fill your pot!)

½ teaspoon chipotle chili powder

salt and pepper, to taste

3 cups dried split peas

more chopped ham, if desired

**1**   Heat the oil in a large stockpot over medium-high heat until the pot is nice and hot. Sauté the onion, carrots, and celery until softened, about 10 minutes. Stir in the minced garlic and cook for about 30 seconds, until very fragrant.

**2**   Nestle the ham hock or bone into the pot and pour the chicken stock in (and enough water, if needed, to cover the ham hock). Stir in the chipotle powder (or smoked paprika if you don't like spice!) and salt and pepper, bring to a boil, and then reduce the heat to low, cover, and simmer for 2–3 hours.

(Okay, please don't let that ham hock scare you! They are cheap, wonderful, and available at the meat counter of every grocery store. You will be so glad you tried them! If you make this after the holidays and have a ham bone in your freezer, go ahead and use that instead. If there's not enough meat clinging on either, then add some more chopped ham to the soup if you like a meatier soup like we do!)

**3**   Remove the ham hock, cutting off any of the meat that is still on the bone, and return the meat to the pot. Taste the broth for seasonings and add more salt and pepper, if needed. (If you want more ham in your soup, now is the time to add it!)

**4**   Stir in the dried split peas and bring the soup back up to a boil. Reduce the heat to low again and simmer, with the lid off, until the split peas are soft and broken down, at least 1 hour.

**5**   Serve hot with lots of crusty french bread for dipping, and a sprinkle of truffle salt if you want to make this extra special! It doesn't get much better than that!

If you want to make this ahead, or if you just like a very thick split pea soup, cook the soup up to this point, and then chill overnight in the fridge. Reheat on the stovetop when you are ready to serve, and you will have a much thicker soup. If you serve this soup the day you make it, it will be thinner but still delicious! I never have the patience to wait until day 2 to eat some, which is why I like this nice big batch of soup! Eat some the first day, chill, and reheat another day for thick leftovers!

*Serves 8–10*

# the best homemade greek salad

*I could eat this salad every single day. And I mean that. It almost drives my husband crazy when we eat this (he loves it too!), because I can't stop saying, "Mmm . . . I could eat this every day!" over and over again.*

*Every time I take a bite and the "mmmm . . ." comes out loud enough for him to hear, he interrupts and says, "I know, I know—you could eat this every day!" It's a problem.*

*Except it's really not, because this salad is just plain delicious, super easy to throw together, and incredibly good for you (well, maybe not if you add the bacon)! Try this. You'll want to eat it every day!*

**FOR THE VINAIGRETTE:**

⅓ cup olive oil

¼ cup fresh squeezed lemon juice (from 1–2 lemons)

1 teaspoon dijon mustard

½ teaspoon dried oregano

½ teaspoon pepper

¼ teaspoon salt

**FOR THE SALAD:**

1 large head romaine, chopped

2 handfuls baby spinach, chopped

½ cup thinly sliced red onion

1 cup crumbled feta

1 cup kalamata olives, halved

½ cup sun-dried tomatoes, chopped

½ pound bacon, browned and crumbled, optional

**1**   In a small jar with a tight-fitting lid, measure the vinaigrette ingredients (lemon juice, olive oil, dijon, and salt and pepper) and shake well to combine. Set aside.

**2**   In a large bowl, layer the salad ingredients.

(This salad can be made up to a day in advance, keeping the dressing separate from the rest. The dressing can be made *several* days in advance. Let the dressing sit at room temperature for a bit before tossing with the salad to let the olive oil soften back up!)

**3**   When you are ready to serve, pour about half of the well-shaken dressing over the salad and toss until lightly coated all over. Add more dressing, a little at a time, until you are happy with how much it's coated!

*Serves 2–4*

# slow cooker french onion beef soup  🌿GF

*Do you love french onion soup as much as I do? Do you look for it on restaurant menus and secretly cheer when you find it? Then I just might be your new best friend!*

*Not only is this french onion soup loaded with wonderful bites of tender beef, it is also incredibly easy and delicious! Serve this proudly to the meat lovers in your life. Enjoy!*

4 tablespoons butter

4 large sweet onions

3 large cloves garlic, minced

2 tablespoons balsamic vinegar

1 tablespoon worcestershire sauce

3 tablespoons flour

1 cup beer

6 cups beef stock

2 tablespoons fresh thyme

salt & pepper, to taste

small (1½ pound or so) lean roast (or 1½ pounds of beef stew meat)

french bread, thick sliced

shredded gruyère cheese

**1**  Turn your (6-quart or bigger) slow cooker on HIGH, place the butter in the bottom, cover and let it heat while you cut the onions in half and then thinly slice them and prep the rest of your ingredients!

**2**  When the butter is melted, stir in the sliced onions, the garlic, balsamic vinegar, and worcestershire sauce. Cover again and cook on HIGH for 1 hour, until the onions are soft and starting to brown on the edges.

**3**  Dump in the flour, stirring well to coat, and cook for 5 minutes. (If you want, you can stop here, place the whole thing into the fridge overnight, and continue on in the morning!) Salt and pepper the stew meat generously and nestle into the slow cooker with the beer, beef stock, thyme, and a touch more salt and pepper, depending on how salty your beef stock is. Cook on LOW heat for 8–12 hours, until the meat is tender, remove it from the pot, shred it up into bite-sized bits, and return to the soup.

**4**  There are two ways to serve this soup! The traditional french onion soup way is to ladle the soup into oven-proof bowls and top with a thick slice of french bread and a generous sprinkle of shredded gruyère cheese. Place the bowls on a baking sheet and broil until the cheese is melted and golden, watching carefully.

**5**  An easier way to serve this for a crowd is to leave the soup in the slow cooker and make a tray of cheese toasts to serve on top of each bowl. Preheat the oven to 450°F. Place thick slices of french bread or thick sliced baguettes in an even layer on a rimmed baking sheet. Top generously with shredded gruyère cheese. Bake for 5–10 minutes, watching carefully, until the cheese is melted and golden, and let everyone grab their own to top their bowls of soup or just to dip and eat as they go!

*Serves 6–8*

# teriyaki-shop-style salad (creamy sesame salad dressing)

GF

*I have a deep deep love for teriyaki shop spicy chicken teriyaki, and more specifically for the creamy, sweet sesame dressing that comes on the salad that accompanies it! Am I the only one obsessed with such a simple salad? I hope not!*

*If you love it as much as I do, you will be happy to know that after many, many trials and errors, I have come up with the closest match I can find, and the best simple salad I've ever eaten! This one really doesn't need more than lettuce and maybe a few thin sliced carrots for decoration. The dressing is the star!*

1 cup mayonnaise

3 tablespoons rice vinegar

2 tablespoons sugar

2 tablespoons sesame oil

1 tablespoon soy sauce

1 clove finely minced garlic (or ¼ teaspoon garlic powder)

lots of black pepper

**1**   Place all the ingredients in a jar with a tight-fitting lid and shake well until completely blended. Taste for seasoning (adding a bit of salt or pepper if needed!) and serve over a simple green salad!

This dressing can be made ahead and stored in the fridge for up to 2 weeks! Shake well before serving.

*Serves 6~8*

SOUPS & SALADS

# tomato-feta pasta salad ⬦GFA

*I feel like I need to make a disclaimer here right away. This absolutely does NOT have to be a pasta salad! If you just plain want an amazing tomato salad or bruschetta topping, this amazing summer salad is your jam!*

*The pasta just makes this more of a meal, which is why I love it. I could eat this by the bowlful all summer long. Nothing tastes more like summer to me than this beautiful tomato salad. Pasta or no, you will love this!*

1 pound short noodles, cooked according to package directions

½ cup extra virgin olive oil

2 lbs cherry or grape tomatoes, halved (about 3 pints or 6 cups)

½ large red onion, finely chopped

⅓ cup white wine vinegar

1 pound french goat's milk feta, diced*

½ cup chopped fresh basil leaves

½ cup chopped fresh italian flat-leaf parsley

salt and pepper, to taste

**1**   Drain the noodles and toss them in a large bowl with the olive oil. Set aside to cool. When the pasta is cool to the touch, gently toss in the rest of the ingredients, tasting a few bites to see if you need more salt and pepper or vinegar.

*You can use regular feta if that's all you can find, but if you can find feta with goat's milk, you will absolutely love it. And a cube of feta will make better chunks for this salad than little crumbles in a tub!

This is a great salad to make a day in advance! Just leave out the fresh herbs and refrigerate the tossed pasta salad. Take it out of the fridge a few hours before serving and gently toss in the fresh herbs just before you are ready to dig in!

*Serves 6~8*

# slow cooker smoky ham & bean soup  GF

*Nothing but classic, simple comfort food here. This is incredibly quick and easy to throw together and fills every comfort-food-craving piece of your soul.*

*Busy, stressful winter days need this soup. Yes, I said* need*!*

1 tablespoon olive oil or bacon grease

1 large onion, chopped

3 large carrots, chopped

3–4 celery stalks, chopped

3 large cloves garlic, minced

2 cups diced ham

4 (15-ounce) cans beans, drained

4 cups chicken stock

1 (14.5-ounce) can diced tomatoes

2 teaspoons ground cumin

1 teaspoon chipotle chile powder, or smoked paprika

salt and pepper, to taste

**1** Heat the oil or bacon grease in the slow cooker on HIGH while you chop up the veggies. Stir in the chopped onions, carrots, celery, and garlic to coat, and then stir in the rest of the ingredients.

**2** Cook on LOW 8–12 hours.

A little slow cooker tip for you—never open the slow cooker to check on the food. Every time you open the lid, 30 minutes should be added onto the cook time!

*Serves 8–10*

# slow cooker cabbage patch soup 🌱GF

*It was always a good day, growing up, when we walked in the door to the smell of this amazing soup. It meant home, fall, and comfort. I could eat bowl after bowl of this hearty soup and not get tired of it . . . and I still can!*

*We grew up calling this soup "hamburger soup," but that name just doesn't do it justice. After much deliberation (and input from my family and friends!), we have decided to rename this delicious, hearty soup "cabbage patch soup." (Don't worry—my mom approves of the new name!)*

*Full of cabbage, beef, veggies, and a rich, tomato broth, this soup has no rival. It is quick, easy, and a total crowd pleaser!*

2 pounds ground beef

½ teaspoon garlic powder

1 large onion, chopped

1 cup chopped celery

¾1 head of cabbage, chopped

1 pound (about 3⅓ cups) frozen sweet corn

1 (64-ounce ) bottle V8 veggie tomato juice (I like spicy; use what you like!)

salt and pepper, to taste

1   In a large skillet, brown the ground beef over medium-high heat, seasoning it with salt, pepper, and the garlic powder, breaking it up into bite-sized chunks as it cooks. Once it is browned, remove it and drain off all but about 1 tablespoon of the grease (if there was hardly any, add a bit of olive oil to the pan!). Sauté the chopped onion and celery in the pan, scraping up the bits of flavor on the bottom, until soft.

2   Transfer the meat, onions, celery, and the rest of the ingredients (cabbage shrinks down substantially, so pack in the pot!) to a large slow cooker and cook on LOW for 8–12 hours.

If you would rather make this on the stove, dump all the ingredients into a large pot, bring to a boil and reduce the heat to LOW, cover, and simmer for 2–3 hours, or as long as you'd like!

If you want to make this even easier to throw together, you can brown the meat, onions, and celery ahead of time and transfer them to a freezer-safe bag. Freeze for up to 3 months, and you are one step closer to an easy, delicious, no-fuss meal!

Optional: serve with noodles.

*Serves 8–10*

# mexican chicken corn chowder ⊾GF

*I wish I could have you all over for dinner and give you a big ol' hug for reading this book. It just makes my heart so happy.*

*And if I did have you over? This is most likely what you would be served. This is my all-time favorite, crowd pleasing, company dish. It is rich, special, and packed full of flavor. It is different and comforting all at the same time. With a big green salad and a loaf of french bread, dinner is served and about as easy as it gets!*

*Give this a try and see why it's my favorite!*

4 tablespoons butter

2 pounds chicken, diced

1 large onion, chopped

2 large cloves garlic, minced

4 cups chicken stock

2 teaspoons ground cumin

2 (14.75-ounce) cans cream-style corn

2 (4-ounce) cans diced green chiles

4 cups half & half

4 cups shredded mexican cheese blend (or monterey jack)

salt and pepper, to taste

2 cups fresh salsa (good quality!)

fresh cilantro

diced avocado

**1**  In a large pot, melt the butter over medium-high heat until the pot is nice and hot. Add in the chicken, season it with salt and pepper, and brown it on all sides. Remove the chicken to a plate.

**2**  Into the hot pot, add the onions and sauté for about 5 minutes, scraping the bottom with a wooden spoon to get up any bits from the chicken. Add in the garlic and cook for 30 seconds, or until very fragrant.

**3**  Return the chicken to the pot (along with any juices that have accumulated on the plate!) and add in the chicken stock and cumin. Simmer until the stock has reduced by about half, and then turn the heat down to LOW and stir in the corn and chiles.

If you want to get a head start, stir in the corn and chiles and let cool before placing in the fridge overnight. (Or you can let it simmer at a very low heat on the stove all day!) You can even freeze the base at that point, to thaw and reheat with the rest of the ingredients another time!

**4**  Stir in the half & half and the shredded cheese, and stir occasionally until the soup is nice and hot and the cheese is melted. Stir in the salsa and taste for salt seasoning before serving. Top with chopped fresh cilantro and chopped avocado, if desired, and serve with lots of fresh bread to sop up every bit of yum!

This soup tastes great reheated, and it is almost impossible to eat just one bowl, so make the whole batch, even if you don't think you need that much!

*Serves 6~8*

# appetizers, snacks & sides

# peanut butter & jelly puffs

*These sweet little kid-friendly treats are such a fun twist on the usual peanut butter and jelly. They are simple enough to be loved by everyone and cute enough to be served at a party.*

*These puffs are best served room temperature, so make them whenever you have a few minutes and you've got a fun after-school snack your kids will love or a fun little party treat!*

1 sheet frozen puff pastry

about ⅓ cup smooth peanut butter

about ½ cup freezer jam

powdered sugar

**1**   Thaw one sheet of frozen puff pastry according to package directions. Preheat the oven to 400°F and line a baking sheet with parchment.

**2**   Unfold the thawed puff pastry, cut it into small rectangles (as big as you'd like!), and separate the rectangles onto a parchment-lined baking sheet.

**3**   With a small paring knife, gently score through the top half of the dough (not all the way through!) a smaller rectangle into the center of each piece. Place a dollop of peanut butter into the center of each piece, being careful to stay inside the smaller rectangle.

**4**   Bake for 15 minutes, until puffed and golden. Remove from the oven, let cool until room temperature, and then top with a dollop of your favorite freezer jam and sprinkle with powdered sugar!

*Serves 6~8*

# artichoke dip puff pastry bites

*It doesn't get much easier than these simple 4-ingredient appetizers. Perfect for a cocktail party or a fancy snack while you lounge and watch a movie. Also, they're great for potlucks! You really can't go wrong with these grab-and-eat bites!*

*You can use leftover Rosemary Bacon Artichoke Dip from this book or your favorite store-bought artichoke dip for the filling. Whatever you have on hand is fine!*

1 sheet frozen puff pastry

about 1 cup cold artichoke dip

freshly grated parmesan cheese

2–3 tablespoons olive oil

**1**  Thaw one sheet of frozen puff pastry according to package directions. Preheat the oven to 400°F and line a baking sheet with parchment.

**2**  Unfold the thawed puff pastry, cut it into small rectangles (as big as you'd like!), and separate the rectangles onto a parchment-lined baking sheet.

**3**  With a small paring knife, gently score through the top half of the dough (not all the way through!) a smaller rectangle into the center of each piece. Place a generous dollop of the artichoke dip into the center of each piece, being careful to stay inside the smaller rectangle. Sprinkle the tops with a generous dusting of parmesan.

**4**  Bake for 15 minutes, until puffed and golden. Remove from the oven, drizzle lightly with olive oil, and serve hot, warm, or room temperature!

*Serves 6~8*

# fresh cranberry apple sauce ⊱GF

*I learned this wonderful dish from my cousin Kay. I spent a few Thanksgivings with my Minnesota family when I was a teenager, and Kay always made this tart, fresh cranberry sauce that was my favorite part of the Thanksgiving feast.*

*No Thanksgiving is complete without this dish now, and even to this day, every time I make this, I think of her and remember the holidays I spent with my sweet midwest family!*

*This is a great, fresh addition to your holiday table that is sure to win over as many hearts in your family as it has in mine. But with a few bags of fresh cranberries in your freezer, you can make this anytime!*

1 pound (5 cups) fresh cranberries (frozen is fine!)

2 large granny smith apples, quartered and cored (leave the skins on!)

1 large orange, zested and juiced

¾–1 cup sugar, to taste

1 teaspoon ground cardamom, optional

This is a 2-step process that needs a large food processor with shredding attachments.

**1**  Run the fresh cranberries and the apples through the shredder, dumping into a big bowl as needed. When it's all "shredded," dump out the food processor, switch out to the regular processing blade and transfer the cranberries and apples back into the processor.

**2**  Pulse several times until very finely chopped (this should look almost like ground beef texture—bad analogy, I know!), and then transfer to a large bowl and stir in the orange zest, juice, and sugar (and the cardamom, if using), to taste. Stir well and chill for at least 24 hours and up to 5 days in the fridge to let the flavors meld and the sugar dissolve. Taste and add a bit more sugar, if needed!

*Serves 10–12*

# loaded jalapeño popper dip ⬧GFA

*Do you love jalapeño poppers as much as I do? I could eat this dip all day, every day. But if you've ever tried making traditional poppers at home, you know they are not a 5-minute process. They are delicious, but they take a bit of work.*

*This party-pleasing dip takes all the work out of great poppers and leaves all the flavor. So worth the few minutes to throw together, and it tastes even better if you make it a few days in advance and let the flavors meld in the fridge. It doesn't get much better than that!*

1 (8-ounce) brick cream cheese, softened

¼ cup sour cream

¼ cup mayonnaise

1 small (4-ounce) can fire-roasted diced green chiles

¼ pound bacon

3–4 medium-large fresh jalapeño peppers,* seeded and finely chopped

2 green onion stalks, white and light green parts, chopped (about 2 tablespoons)

¾ cup freshly grated parmesan cheese, divided (½ cup + ¼ cup)

¼ cup panko bread crumbs

*Take all the seeds and white membranes out of the jalapeños and then taste a tiny bit of each one to see how many you want to use. Jalapeño peppers vary greatly in their spiciness, so I can't tell you exactly how much to put in your dip. Err on the side of less though, if you're not sure—you can always add more spice (crushed red pepper flakes at the end will taste great!), but you don't want this to be so screaming hot you can't enjoy it!

**1** In a large bowl, beat together the cream cheese, sour cream, and mayo until smooth (you can use a stand mixer or hand mixer for this).

**2** Brown the bacon in a large skillet until dark and crisp. Cut up or crumble and add to the cream cheese mixture. In the hot skillet with bacon grease left in it, sauté the chopped jalapeño peppers for a few minutes, until soft.

**3** Scoop the jalapeños out onto a paper-towel-lined plate, and then dump them into the cream cheese mixture with the chopped green onions and ½ cup of the grated parmesan.

You can continue on at this point, or you can cover this mixture and place it in the fridge overnight or up to 3 days.

**4** When you are going to serve, preheat the oven to 400°F, spread the mixture into a shallow baking dish (a pie plate will work well), and sprinkle the top with the remaining ¼ cup parmesan and the panko crumbs.

**5** Bake until golden and bubbly, about 20–30 minutes.

**6** Serve warm with lots of tortilla chips for dipping!

Make this dip up to 3 days in advance, maybe even longer. Let soften a bit at room temperature so you can spread it into a baking dish and sprinkle with the panko and parmesan before baking until golden and bubbly!

*Serves 6~8*

APPETIZERS, SNACKS & SIDES

# bacon rosemary artichoke dip 🌱GF

*I just can't stop thinking about/making/eating this dip. It is a total game changer in the dip arena. Trust me, whip this one up and you will be as hooked as I am. I could almost cry thinking about how much I love it! (I may have a problem.)*

*A few times a year, we make a point to go to one of our favorite restaurants out here on the Olympic Peninsula—LD's Woodfire Grill (also known as Wildfire)—and spoil ourselves. This year, it was for my birthday, and as usual, the food did not disappoint.*

*We ordered artichoke dip as an appetizer, and I was completely blown away. The rosemary was so surprising and absolutely beyond glorious! We quickly polished it off, and I just couldn't stop thinking about it. So into the kitchen I went, and this is what came out. I added bacon because, well, bacon!*

*This makes a big batch, because I've got a big family, and who doesn't like to have a great hot dip recipe to share! Feel free to cut this in half for a smaller crowd, or bake up half of it one night and the rest a few days later. That's the plan I usually use!*

2 (8-ounce) bricks cream cheese, softened

½ cup sour cream

½ cup mayo

½ cup sautéed chopped jalapeños (or an 8-ounce can diced green chiles)

1 cup homemade bacon bits (about ½ pound bacon browned and crumbled)

2 (13.75-ounce) cans quartered artichoke hearts in water, drained and roughly chopped

2 tablespoons finely chopped fresh rosemary leaves

1½ cups freshly grated parmesan cheese, divided (1 cup + ½ cup)

crushed red pepper flakes, optional

garlic bread, for serving

**1**  In a large bowl, stir together the cream cheese, sour cream, and mayo until smooth.

**2**  Stir in the sautéed jalapeños, bacon, artichoke hearts, rosemary, and 1 cup of the parmesan until well mixed.

If you are making this ahead, cover well and place in the fridge overnight, or up to a week. It definitely tastes better as it sits, so plan to make it at least a day ahead, if you can!

**3**  When you are ready to serve, preheat the oven to 400°F, spread the mixture into a shallow baking dish (9×13" or two pie plates are good!), and sprinkle the remaining ½ cup of parmesan cheese over the tops.

**4**  Bake for 20–30 minutes, until the dip is golden and bubbly and hot. Serve warm with crushed red pepper flakes for people who like more heat, and lots of garlic bread for serving!

*Serves 6~8*

# homemade mediterranean-style hummus

*When I got married, I moved to a small town a few hours away from Seattle where I grew up. It was quite an adjustment, and one of the things I missed the most were the variety of grocery and specialty stores I was used to having easy access to before.*

*The first few years, I made the trip back to the city as often as I could to stock my fridge and my pantry with my favorite treats. Then I started to realize how much time and money I was wasting when I could probably just learn to make some of those things at home.*

*Enter this hummus. Now, this is not just any hummus. It's not exactly what you're probably used to, unless you've had Trader Joe's Mediterranean-Style Hummus. This homemade version is bright and lemony and absolutely addicting!*

2 (15-ounce) cans garbanzo beans, drained and rinsed (about 3 cups)

1 large garlic clove

6 tablespoons good-quality extra-virgin olive oil

2 tablespoons tahini

1¼ teaspoons salt

zest of 1 large lemon

juice of 2 large lemons

¼ teaspoon ground cumin

½ teaspoon crushed red pepper flakes

about ½ cup hot water

**1**  Place the garlic clove in the food processor and pulse a few times to mince.

**2**  Dump in the rest of the ingredients, except for the hot water, and run for 3–4 minutes.

**3**  After the first 30 seconds or so, stream in the water while the processor is still running until you have reached your desired consistency, and then continue to process until the hummus is very smooth and creamy.

**4**  Taste for seasonings and consistency, adding a bit more water if needed. The hummus will set up a bit as it chills in the fridge, so make it slightly runnier than you think you'd like.

**5**  Pour the hummus into a container and chill overnight, or up to 5 days. The longer it sits, the more the flavors will meld and blossom!

**6**  Before serving, drizzle with a bit more extra-virgin olive oil and sprinkle with crushed red pepper flakes, pine nuts, and chopped parsley if you'd like!

**7**  Serve with all your favorite dippers—pita chips, veggies, rice crackers, fingers, and so on!

Don't freeze this hummus, but make it up to a week in advance. It tastes even better as it sits!

*Serves 6~8*

# simple sourdough stuffing

*Everyone has their favorite Thanksgiving side dish, and this is one of mine.*

*Second only to my fresh cranberry apple sauce, this buttery sourdough stuffing is the perfect accompaniment to the moist turkey and rich mashed potatoes and gravy.*

*Does anyone else love Thanksgiving food as much as I do?!*

1 large loaf sourdough bread, cubed and left to dry overnight

1½ cups butter

1½ tablespoons poultry seasoning

1 large onion, chopped

2 cups chopped celery

2 teaspoons salt

1 teaspoon pepper

2–3 cups chicken stock

**1**   Preheat the oven to 350°F. Butter a 9×13" baking dish. Set aside.

**2**   Heat the butter and poultry seasoning in a large skillet over medium-high heat. Add in the onions and celery and sauté for 5–10 minutes, until soft. Add in about ½–⅔ of the stale bread cubes (as much as your pan can hold) and sauté them in the butter until starting to turn golden and absorb the butter.

**3**   Stir in the rest of the bread and dump the mixture into the buttered dish. Pour 2–3 cups of chicken stock all over the bread (more if you like wetter dressing, less if you like drier dressing!) and place in the oven to bake for 30–45 minutes until golden.

You can stuff some of this into your turkey if you'd like! And another way to make this ahead is to place everything in a slow cooker instead of into the buttered pan and heat on LOW for as long as you need until you serve it!

*Serves 8–10*

# slow cooker calico beans  GF

*Calico beans are a satisfying cross between chili, baked beans, and a sloppy joe filling.*

*Full of a homemade barbecue–style sauce, lots of meat, bacon, and tender beans, these calico beans are meaty, tangy, salty, and deliciously perfect for any barbecue, picnic, or potluck you are heading to!*

1 pound ground beef, browned and drained

1 pound bacon, cooked and crumbled

1 large onion, chopped

½ cup ketchup

⅓ cup firmly packed brown sugar

1 tablespoon apple cider vinegar

1 tablespoon worcestershire sauce

1 teaspoon yellow mustard

1 teaspoon salt

½ teaspoon crushed red pepper flakes

1 (15-ounce) can tomato sauce

6 cups cooked mixed beans (if you like to use dried)

OR

2 (15-ounce) cans white beans, drained

1 (15-ounce) can kidney beans, drained

**1**  Combine all ingredients in a large slow cooker, and stir gently until combined. Cook on LOW for at least 4 hours and up to 8 hours.

If you like to use dried beans, you can make them ahead of time and freeze them in already portioned out amounts in freezer bags, making this almost as easy as opening a can for a fraction of the cost!

*Serves 12–16*

63

# rich & creamy fully loaded make-ahead mashed potatoes

**GF**

*These are not your average, quick, weeknight mashed potatoes. These are your "impress the crowds"or "win over the guy" mashed potatoes. These are your big-deal mashed potatoes that take a bit of time to make but can be made several days in advance and are worth every second.*

*Rich, creamy, whipped, and buttery, it just doesn't get much better than these. If you are making a big meal (think Thanksgiving, with all the trimmings!), you can leave out the bacon, green onions and cheddar cheese if you'd like. But if you're serving a grilled steak, or a simple roast chicken, these are the potatoes for you. They serve a crowd, and they are everyone's favorite!*

5 pounds russet potatoes, washed, peeled, and cut into 1" pieces

1 (8-ounce) package cream cheese, room temperature

1 cup sour cream

1 cup heavy cream

1 cup cooked, crumbled bacon

1 bunch green onions, chopped

2 cups shredded cheddar cheese

salt and pepper

½ cup butter, melted

**1** Place the potatoes into a large pot. Cover with cold water and let sit for 10 minutes, and then rinse and fill to about 1" above the potatoes with fresh cold water.

While the potatoes are soaking, pull out the sour cream and cream cheese so it can warm up a bit to room temperature while you continue with the recipe. In a small saucepan, heat the butter with the heavy cream over medium-low heat until the butter is melted. Turn the burner off and leave the mixture there to stay warm.

**2** Bring the potatoes to a boil over high heat, add a tablespoon or so of salt to the water when it's boiling and cook until fork tender, about 15 minutes. Drain into a colander and rinse again quickly with cold water.

**3** Place the cream cheese into a stand mixer bowl and beat until smooth. Using a potato ricer, press the potatoes through into the bowl of the stand mixer on top of the cream cheese. Once they are all in there, turn the mixer on low and stream in the warm cream until the mixture is smooth. Mix in the sour cream until combined.

**4** Stir in the bacon bits, chopped green onions, and shredded cheddar cheese, along with salt and pepper, to taste.

**5** Spread into a 9×13" baking dish and drizzle evenly with the melted butter. You can bake this now, or you can cover tightly and place in the fridge to bake up to 3 days later.

**6** Preheat the oven to 350°F. Bake for 30–60 minutes, depending on if the potatoes are chilled or still warm, until heated through and golden on top!

*Serves 12–16*

Main Dishes

# main dishes

# rosemary chicken pot pie ⏷GFA

*There is just something so incredibly comforting about a homemade chicken pot pie. Yes, it requires a bit more work than throwing together a casserole, but I believe that not many foods say "I love you" like a homemade pot pie.*

*The greatest thing about any pot pie? They can be made ahead of time, when you're in the mood to putz around the kitchen, and then you can bake one and have an incredibly special meal anytime!*

Your favorite recipe for a double-crust pie dough*

2 tablespoons bacon grease

2 tablespoons butter

1½ cups chopped onions

2 cups chopped carrots

1 cup chopped celery

1 cup diced raw potatoes

2 large cloves garlic, minced

4 tablespoons flour

3 cups chicken stock

1 cup heavy cream

3 cups diced, cooked chicken

2 tablespoons chopped fresh rosemary

½ pound bacon, cooked and crumbled (about ¾ cup), grease reserved

½ teaspoon onion powder

¼ teaspoon garlic powder

¼ teaspoon crushed red pepper flakes

salt and pepper, to taste

*My favorite recipe for pie dough is from Kate McDermott's *The Art of the Pie*. You can find it online or in her cookbook! Use what you love. And if you don't want to make your own pie dough, a store bought refrigerated dough will work in a pinch!

**1**  Roll out one round of dough and ease it gently into the bottom of a deep dish pie plate. Place the dish in the fridge while you make the filling.

**2**  In a large skillet, melt together 2 tablespoons bacon grease and 2 tablespoons butter (if you don't use bacon grease, feel free to substitute with more butter or coconut oil!) over medium-high heat.

**3**  Toss in the onions, carrots, celery, and potatoes and sauté for 10–15 minutes, until the vegetables are starting to get soft and golden. Stir in the garlic and sauté another minute. Sprinkle the flour over the vegetables and stir to coat. Continue to cook and stir, until the flour is absorbed and toasty.

**4**  Slowly stir in the chicken stock and bring to a boil, stirring constantly and scraping the bottom of the pan to get up all the yummy bits. Simmer until the stock has reduced by half. Stir in the heavy cream and simmer on LOW until thick.

**5**  Turn off the heat and stir in the chicken and spices. Taste for seasoning and add more as needed. Let this mixture cool for a bit (until it is warm, but not hot if you plan to cook the pie immediately, or until it is cool if you plan on freezing the pie to cook later!), and then pour into the bottom crust, heaping it up as needed in the center of the dish.

**6**  Place the filled crust back into the fridge while you roll out the top dough and then bring the pie back out and transfer the dough, gently to the top of the pie. Trim the edges to about 1" over the edge of the plate, tuck under the edge of the bottom crust, and press firmly around the edges to crimp the pie (sealing in the filling).

**7**  Cut a few slits in the top to let steam out, brush the top of the crust all over with a bit of egg wash (1 egg lightly beaten with a tablespoon of cold water), and sprinkle generously with coarsely ground salt and pepper.

**8**  Place the pie back in the fridge while you place a baking sheet on the lower third rack of the oven and preheat to 425°F. After 30 minutes, place the chilled pie on the preheated baking sheet.

**9**  After 15 minutes, reduce the heat to 350°F and cook for 60–90 minutes, until the crust is deep golden brown (not burnt!) and the filling is hot and bubbling. (If the crust starts to brown too fast, cover loosely with foil until done.)

**10**  Let cool for 10–15 minutes before serving! The hotter the pot pie is when you serve it, the "messier" the slices will be, but they will still taste amazing—just use bowls!

*If you plan on making this ahead of time, after it is all assembled, wrap well with plastic wrap and foil and freeze. When you are ready to bake it, pull it out of the freezer and remove the wrapping. Place it on the counter to thaw for 30 minutes while you preheat the oven. Bake according to the directions above, adding extra time at the end as needed, until the pot pie is hot and the crust is golden!*

If you are just making this one or two days ahead and don't want to freeze it, you can par-bake it (meaning, until very lightly golden and not all the way done!), cool completely, cover tightly with foil, and refrigerate for up to 3 days. Preheat the oven to 350°F and bake again until hot, very golden, and bubbly, about 60 minutes or so!

*Serves 6~8*

MAIN DISHES

# freezer-friendly chicken broccoli quinoa casserole

GFA

*I grew up eating this mouth-watering chicken broccoli casserole. Rich, creamy, cheesy, and flavorful, but also packed with broccoli. I think we thought we were getting a healthy meal with this one because of all that green.*

*Now, I wouldn't necessarily call this healthy or eat it every day, but it is the most amazing comfort-food meal. And I have made it a little less guilt-inducing with super easy homemade cream of chicken soup and a dose of quinoa to punch it up with a bit more nutrients (and carbs to stretch this meal a bit for my big family of little bottomless tummies)!*

*This is a company meal. Whip a few up when you're in the mood to cook on a lazy afternoon, and then store them in the freezer to pull out when you have company coming over, or friends who could use a meal dropped off at their door. Heat it up and toss together a big green salad to go with it, and dinner is ready!*

**FOR THE HOMEMADE CONDENSED CREAM OF CHICKEN SOUP:**

2 cups chicken stock

1 teaspoon poultry seasoning

½ teaspoon onion powder

½ teaspoon garlic powder

½ teaspoon pepper

¼ teaspoon salt

¼ teaspoon turmeric

½ cup lowfat milk

½ cup heavy cream

¾ cup flour

**FOR THE CASSEROLE:**

3 cups homemade condensed cream of chicken soup (or use 2 cans store-bought)

1 cup lowfat milk

⅔ cup mayonnaise

¼ cup fresh squeezed lemon or lime juice (2 large lemons or 4 small limes)

1½ teaspoons curry powder

½ teaspoon salt

½ teaspoon pepper

½ teaspoon crushed red pepper flakes

pinch of nutmeg

2½ cups shredded cheese blend (mexican or italian works well!)

8 cups raw, chopped bite-sized broccoli florets

4 cups chopped cooked chicken

2 cups cooked, cooled quinoa

1 cup shredded sharp cheddar cheese

**TO MAKE THE HOMEMADE CREAM OF CHICKEN SOUP:**

**1** In a medium pan, whisk together the chicken stock and spices and bring to a boil over medium-high heat.

**2** While that is coming to a boil, in a small bowl, whisk together the milk, cream, and flour until very smooth (no flour lumps remaining).

**3** When the stock comes to a boil, turn the heat down to medium, and slowly whisk in the flour and milk mixture until well blended. Continue to cook, whisking constantly, until the soup is very very thick (like a can of condensed soup!).

**4** Let cool before using in your recipe. (This makes about 3 cups, or 2 cans of condensed cream of chicken soup.)

**TO MAKE THE CASSEROLE:**

**1** Preheat the oven to 350°F (if you are baking this immediately, instead of freezing for another day!). Butter a 9×13" baking dish and set aside.

**2** In a large bowl, whisk together the condensed soup, milk, mayo, lemon juice, and spices until smooth. Stir in the shredded cheese blend, broccoli, chicken, and quinoa and combine until the mixture is all evenly coated.

**3** Dump this into the buttered baking dish and top with the cup of shredded cheddar. Bake for 30–45 minutes,* until the mixture is hot and bubbly and the cheese is melted and golden on top!

*Unless you are going to freeze this, cover well with plastic wrap and foil and freeze for up to 3 months! Remove from the freezer while you preheat the oven to 350°F and then bake for about an hour, or until the casserole is very hot and the cheese is golden. If it starts to brown on top before the inside is hot, cover loosely with foil until it's done!

*Serves 8–10*

# cashew chicken and brown rice casserole ⊗GF

*Rich, creamy, cheesy, and oh so good, this is everything you love about a classic comfort-food casserole, kicked up a bit with some buttery cashews and a hit of lemon juice. It's sure to be a quick favorite!*

4 cups chopped, cooked chicken

2½ cups chopped celery

1½ cups coarsely chopped cashews

1 cup mayonnaise

1 cup sour cream

1 cup chicken stock

½ of a large onion, very finely chopped

½ cup brown rice

¼ cup fresh squeezed lemon juice (from 2 large lemons)

1½ cups shredded cheddar cheese, divided (1 cup + ½ cup)

**1**  Preheat the oven to 350°F.  Butter a 9×13" baking dish and set aside.

**2**  In a large bowl, stir together all of the casserole ingredients, except the last ½ cup of shredded cheddar. Dump the mixture into the buttered baking dish and sprinkle evenly with the remaining cheese.

**3**  Cover with foil and bake for 45 minutes, and then remove the foil and continue to bake until golden and the rice is tender (you may need to sneak a tiny taste here!), 20–30 minutes.

**4**  Serve immediately or let cool completely, cover well, and freeze to reheat another day.

This will last in the freezer for up to 3 months, very well wrapped. Heat in a 350°F oven until hot and bubbling!

*Serves 10–12*

# make-ahead pepperoni pizza rolls

*This fun dinner is a huge hit with the kids and kids at heart. It freezes wonderfully and makes a great potluck dish, or a meal to bless a sick friend or a family with a new baby.*

*Swirly and adorable and reminiscent of cinnamon rolls, these are savory instead of sweet, filled with pizza sauce, pepperoni, and cheese, and so, so good! Give them a try the next time you want to wow your kids. They won't be disappointed!*

**FOR THE SAUCE:**

1 tablespoon extra-virgin olive oil

2 large cloves garlic, smashed

1 (15-ounce) can tomato sauce

2 tablespoons dried oregano

1 tablespoon dried rosemary

2 teaspoons dried minced onions

½ teaspoon sugar

½ teaspoon salt

¼–½ teaspoon crushed red pepper flakes (less if you don't like spice!)

**FOR THE DOUGH:**

2 cups evaporated milk (or whole milk)

½ cup butter

2¼ teaspoons (1 packet) active dry yeast

4½ cups flour, divided (4 cups + ½ cup)

1½ teaspoons salt

1 teaspoon garlic powder

½ teaspoon baking powder

½ teaspoon baking soda

**FOR THE FILLING:**

pizza sauce (see above)

shredded mozzarella cheese

pepperoni slices

freshly grated parmesan cheese

**1 FOR THE SAUCE:** In a small pot, heat the olive oil over medium heat until hot, and then sauté the smashed garlic cloves until very fragrant—30 seconds to 1 minute. Stir in the rest of the ingredients, bring to a quick boil, and then reduce the heat to low and simmer. The longer this simmers the better. You can even make a double or triple batch of this and freeze it ahead of time to pull out when you need it!

**2 FOR THE ROLLS:** In a large dutch oven, heat the milk and butter over medium heat, until just starting to simmer around the edges. Turn off the heat, move the pot off the burner, and let it cool to room temperature for about an hour or so.

**3** When the milk is room temperature, sprinkle the yeast on the top and let it sit for a few minutes while you measure out the flour. In a small bowl, stir together ½ cup flour, 1½ teaspoons salt, ½ teaspoon garlic powder, ½ teaspoon baking powder, and ½ teaspoon baking soda and set aside. You will need this later.

**4** In the pot with the milk and yeast, stir in the 4 cups of flour until just well combined. Cover with a clean towel and let rise for about an hour, until the dough is doubled in size. Stir in the little bowl of flour mixture that you mixed up earlier until just well combined, and then recover the bowl with the towel and also the lid and place in the fridge for an hour or two. (You can skip this chilling step—it is not crucial, but it makes the dough easier to roll out and prettier in the end.)

**5** When you are ready to roll out the dough, lightly flour a clean countertop and roll the dough out into a very large rectangle about ¼" thick. Drizzle the top lightly with olive oil, and then spread a fairly thin layer of the pizza sauce evenly over the top. Sprinkle with a generous amount of the shredded mozzarella and then a nice layer of pepperoni slices. Top with a bit of freshly grated parmesan and, starting from the long end, roll the dough up into a log—just like you would for cinnamon rolls—and set it seam side down. Cut the roll into 15 slices and place them cut sides up into a greased 9×13" baking dish.

**6** Cover with a clean towel or plastic wrap and let sit for about 30 minutes, while you preheat the oven to 375°F. The rolls should be quite large by now.

**7** Bake for 15–20 minutes, until the rolls are golden brown on the top and cooked through (you can peek with a sharp knife to see if they are still doughy!), and then serve hot with more warm pizza sauce for dipping!

If you are making these ahead, freeze the finished rolls after they have cooled completely. You can freeze them spread out on a cookie sheet until they are firm and transfer them to a large freezer bag so they can be reheated easily, one or two at a time, as you'd like!

*Serves 8–10*

# slow cooker pineapple coconut chicken curry `GF`

*You might be surprised that this came out of your slow cooker. It's more than your usual soup or stew—and so much fun to eat.*

*Next time you're looking for a slow-cooker dish that's just not the same as all the others, this is the one for you. Make up a batch of rice to serve it with, and a delicious, company-worthy slow cooker dinner is served!*

½ large onion, cut in large chunks

½ large bell pepper, cut in large chunks

2 cloves garlic

1 (15-ounce) can coconut milk

2 tablespoons ketchup

2 teaspoons sriracha sauce

1½ teaspoons salt

1 tablespoon garam masala spice blend

1 tablespoon curry powder

½ teaspoon crushed red pepper flakes, optional for more heat

¼ teaspoon black pepper

2 tablespoons packed chopped fresh basil

4 large frozen chicken breasts

1 can pineapple chunks, drained

**1**  In a large powerful blender or food processor, blend all of the ingredients except the chicken and pineapple chunks, until fairly smooth. (Doesn't have to be perfect, but it is a sauce, not a chunky stew!)

**2**  Place the frozen chicken breasts and the pineapple chunks in the bottom of the slow cooker. Pour the curry sauce all over the top, cover, and turn on LOW for 6–8 hours. When the chicken is cooked through, shred it up with two forks and return it to the sauce.

**3**  If the sauce is not as thick as you would like at this point (and it likely will not be!), make a little cornstarch slurry to thicken it: Mix 1½ tablespoons cornstarch and 2 tablespoons cold water together in a small glass until totally smooth. Stir this into the slow cooker and turn to HIGH for another 15–30 minutes until it is as thick as you'd like.

**4**  Serve the chicken and sauce over your favorite rice!

You can blend the sauce ahead of time and store in the freezer until you need it. Thaw it in the fridge overnight, and then dump it in the slow cooker in the morning and continue with the recipe!

*Serves 6~8*

# slow cooker beef stroganoff GFA

*I have been making this slow cooker stroganoff for years and years. It's one of those dishes that I just start craving when the weather turns and nothing will kick the craving until I make it.*

*Fortunately, it's delicious, and my family loves it too, so there's that!*

**FOR THE HOMEMADE CONDENSED CREAM SOUP:**

½ cup cold milk

⅓ cup flour (all-purpose or gluten-free substitute)

¾ cup beef stock

¼ cup milk

½ teaspoon dried rosemary

½ teaspoon garlic powder

½ teaspoon onion powder

½ teaspoon paprika

½ teaspoon salt

½ teaspoon pepper

**FOR THE REST:**

1½ pounds beef stew meat

2 tablespoons worcestershire sauce

1 tablespoon soy sauce

1 large onion, chopped

2 cloves garlic, minced

1 teaspoon salt

½ teaspoon pepper

1 pound fresh mushrooms, halved or quartered

1 cup beef stock

1 cup sour cream

1 package egg noodles

**1** In a small bowl, whisk together the cold milk and flour until smooth. Set aside.

**2** In a small saucepan, whisk together the rest of the condensed soup ingredients and bring to a boil over medium-high heat. Once the mixture is boiling, slowly stream in the flour and milk slurry, whisking constantly, and continue to boil and whisk until the mixture is VERY thick (remember how thick a can of condensed soup is when you open it!).

**3** In a large slow cooker, stir together the stew meat, worcestershire sauce, and soy sauce until coated. Spread into a layer on the bottom of the slow cooker. Dump the onions and garlic on top of the meat, season with salt and pepper, and then add the mushrooms. Dump in the homemade condensed soup and the beef stock, cover, and cook on LOW for 6–8 hours, until the meat is very tender.

**4** When you are about ready to serve, take off the lid, stir in the sour cream, and turn the heat up to high while you cook the noodles, stirring occasionally. Taste for seasoning and add more salt if needed. You can also stir in some fresh chopped parsley at this point, if you'd like!

**5** Cook the noodles according to package directions, drain, and toss with a bit of butter to keep them from sticking.

**6** Serve the stroganoff over noodles with lots of crusty bread to sop up the sauce!

This condensed soup mixture makes about 1 can or 1½ cups' worth. You can make a much bigger batch and freeze in 1½ cup portions for easy use in any recipe that calls for condensed cream of anything soup! (Substitute chicken stock if you want!)

To make this gluten-free, use gluten-free tamari soy sauce and serve over rice or gluten-free noodles.

*Serves 4–6*

# buffalo chicken baked mac & cheese ⬲GFA

*This guy-pleasing, buffalo chicken–laced mac and cheese has won over many hearts in the past several years.*

*I recently shared some of this with a sweet friend who is a fabulous cook, and her husband's comment was, "There are only two recipes of mac and cheese I like—yours and this one."*

*That's about the highest compliment a mom-chef could ask for*

1 pound short pasta (regular or gluten-free)

**FOR THE CHICKEN MIXTURE:**

4 tablespoons butter

½ large onion, chopped

3 large stalks celery, chopped

4 cups diced cooked chicken

2 large cloves garlic, minced

1 cup bottled buffalo sauce

**FOR THE CHEESE SAUCE:**

2 tablespoons butter

2 tablespoons flour

2 teaspoons dry mustard

1½ cups heavy cream or half & half

1½ cups chicken stock

¼ cup bottled buffalo sauce

4 cups shredded sharp cheddar cheese

2 cups shredded pepper jack cheese

⅔ cup sour cream

**FOR THE TOPPING:**

2 tablespoons butter

¾ cup panko bread crumbs

**1**  Preheat the oven to 350°F. Butter a 9×13" baking dish. Set aside.

**2**  Cook the pasta 1 minute less than package directions, rinse and set aside.

**3**  In a large saucepan, melt 4 tablespoons butter over medium-high heat. Stir in the onions and celery and sauté until soft and starting to brown. Stir in the minced garlic for about 30 seconds, and then the chicken and 1 cup buffalo sauce. Simmer until the sauce has thickened a bit. Dump into a bowl and return the pan to the stove.

**4**  Melt 2 tablespoons butter in that same pan, over medium heat. Sprinkle the flour and dry mustard over the melted butter, stirring constantly, and stir and cook the paste until it is golden and toasty smelling.

**5**  Pour the chicken stock and cream, in a slow stream, into the pan while you whisk constantly until smooth. Stir and simmer until the sauce is thick enough to coat the back of a spoon.

**6**  Turn off the heat and stir in the shredded cheeses and the sour cream until all combined. Stir in the noodles and spread half of the mixture into the buttered baking dish. Spoon the chicken mixture evenly over the top of that, and then top with the rest of the noodle mixture.

**7**  In a small bowl, melt the remaining 2 tablespoons butter and toss it together with the panko. (Use gluten-free bread crumbs or simply omit the topping to make this dish gluten free.) Sprinkle the buttered crumbs over the top of the macaroni and cheese, and bake for 40–50 minutes, until golden and bubbling.

**8**  Serve with celery sticks and blue cheese or ranch dressing, just as you would your favorite hot wings!

This dish can be assembled ahead and frozen instead of baking it. Wrap well and place in the freezer for up to 3 months. Defrost on the counter while you preheat the oven, and then bake at 350°, adding more time as needed until heated through.

*Serves 8–10*

# easy baked mac & cheese GFA

*Well now, this recipe puts the "easy" in mac and ch"easy" . . . Okay, I'll stop. That was way too cheesy. (And now I'm just being ridiculous!)*

*All joking aside, you will love this easy, mostly stovetop-free mac and cheese so much, you may never go back to the little blue box.*

**FOR THE BASE:**

1 pound short pasta, cooked one minute less than package directions

1½ cups diced mozzarella cheese

1½ cups shredded 3-cheese blend

1 tablespoon flour

½ teaspoon salt

½ teaspoon pepper

½ teaspoon smoked paprika, or chipotle chile powder

½ teaspoon dry mustard

½ teaspoon garlic powder

½ teaspoon onion powder

pinch of freshly ground nutmeg

½ cup sour cream

1 large egg

1 cup chicken stock

2 cups half & half

optional: 2 cups diced ham

**FOR THE TOPPING:**

1½ cups shredded 3-cheese blend

2 tablespoons melted butter

¾ cup panko bread crumbs

**1**   Cook the pasta, drain, and set aside. Preheat the oven to 350°F. Butter a 9×13" baking dish.

**2**   In the buttered baking dish, toss together the slightly cooled noodles and the mozzarella and 1½ cups shredded cheese blend. Set aside.

**3**   In a medium bowl, whisk together the rest of the base ingredients until well combined. Pour the mixture over the top of the noodles and cheese in the baking dish.

**4**   Sprinkle evenly with the remaining 1½ cup shredded cheese. In a small bowl, stir together the melted butter and panko bread crumbs until wet. Sprinkle the wet crumbs all over the top of the dish.

**5**   Bake for 45–60 minutes, until the sauce is bubbling and thick and the cheese is golden. (If it starts to get too brown before the sauce is thick, cover lightly with a piece of foil!)

This macaroni and cheese dish can be prepped completely ahead and placed in the fridge for up to 2 days before baking. Perfect for planning ahead for company or a busy weeknight dinner!

*Serves 6~8*

# roasted cauliflower & chicken curry pasta bake ⟨GFA⟩

*I wish I could just give you a taste of this dish, instead of trying to explain its appeal. It is so different—lightly spicy and intense, and yet there is something so familiar and satisfying with the tender chicken, roasted cauliflower, and the creamy, tangy sauce.*

*Cauliflower and curry are not what you usually expect to find in a casserole, but I'm telling you, this is a combo you will keep coming back to!*

**FOR THE ROASTED CAULIFLOWER:**

1 large head cauliflower, cut into bite-sized florets

1 tablespoon melted coconut oil, or coconut-oil spray

½ teaspoon curry powder

½ teaspoon garlic powder

salt and pepper, to taste

juice of one lemon

**FOR THE PASTA:**

¾ pound short pasta, cooked one minute less than package directions

3 cups pre-cooked diced chicken (store-bought rotisserie works great!)

2 cans cream of chicken soup (or homemade!)

1 cup mayonnaise

½ teaspoon curry powder

½ teaspoon cayenne pepper

½ teaspoon garlic

½ teaspoon salt, to taste

½ teaspoon pepper

1 cup shredded sharp cheddar cheese

**1**   Preheat the oven to 500°F. Spread the cauliflower on a rimmed baking sheet. Drizzle the melted coconut oil over the top and toss well, with your hands, to coat. Sprinkle the curry, garlic, and a good amount of salt and pepper over the top and roast for 15–20 minutes, until golden and tender. (Watch carefully at the end so it doesn't burn!) Sprinkle the cauliflower with fresh squeezed lemon juice and transfer to a large bowl. Set aside.

**2**   Reduce the temperature to 350°F and leave the door open for a few minutes to help it cool down. Butter a 9×13" baking dish. Set aside.

**3**   Cook the pasta one minute less than package directions, drain, and add to the bowl with the cauliflower. Add the chicken to this bowl as well, toss everything together, and then dump this mixture into the baking dish. (If it's too much for your baking dish, put some in a smaller one on the side!)

**4**   In a medium bowl, whisk together the rest of the ingredients, except for the shredded cheddar, until smooth. Spread this mixture over the top of the casserole, like frosting, covering the top completely. Sprinkle with the cheddar cheese and bake for 1 hour, or until bubbling and golden!

This dish can be frozen for up to 3 months, wrapped well in plastic or foil. You can freeze it before baking, or after baking when it has cooled completely. Let thaw on the counter for about 30 minutes while you preheat the oven, and then cook until hot throughout. (This will take a few more minutes than if you don't freeze it. Keep an eye on it!)

*Serves 6~8*

MAIN DISHES

# blue cheese & shallot compound butter `GF`

*You know how good steaks taste at nice restaurants, and it always seems hard to recreate that flavor at home? Let me let you in on a little secret—they often top the hot-off-the-grill steaks with butter. Yep, butter. Because butter is beautiful and makes everything taste like heaven.*

*Okay, I know this is cheating a little—being in the "Main Dishes" category of this cookbook—but once you put this flavor-packed butter on your steaks, you will never want to leave it off.*

*So, I guess I could have called this recipe "Steak with Blue Cheese & Shallot Compound Butter," but you can put this on any meat, cooked any way you want.*

*Or, you can just spread it on a slice of sourdough toast—because it really is that good!*

1 cup butter, softened
¼–½ teaspoon crushed red pepper flakes
¼ cup finely chopped shallots
2 large cloves fresh garlic, minced
½ cup blue cheese crumbles
2 tablespoons finely chopped fresh italian parsley
salt and pepper, to taste

**1** Stir the butter, red pepper flakes, shallots, and garlic until it is light, well blended, and soft. Stir in the blue cheese crumbles and the parsley until combined, and the take a little taste. Add as much salt and pepper as you'd like (add a bit, taste, add a bit more—everyone likes a different level of saltiness, so make it how you like!), mixing in gently, and then transfer to large piece of plastic wrap.

**2** Roll the butter gently into a log, wrapped well in the plastic wrap, place in a freezer bag, and place in the fridge or freezer until firm. Slice off some whenever you'd like and top steaks, chicken, and so on!

This butter will keep in the fridge for 1–2 weeks and in the freezer for up to 3 months! No need to thaw—just slice or break off chunks and place on top of a hot steak to melt!

*Serves 8–12*

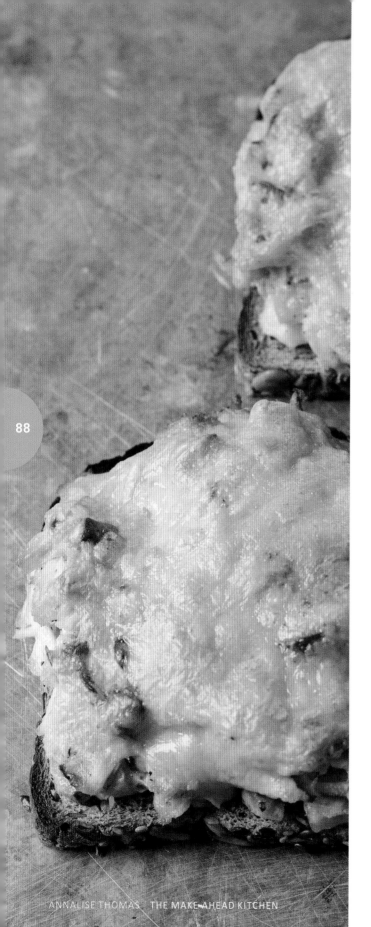

# the best tuna salad for sandwiches & melts ☺GF

*Many years ago, I worked at a sweet little café that had the best tuna melts I had ever had. It was one of the most popular items on the lunch menu, and I can still vividly remember the taste.*

*I love recreating these tuna melts for my friends and family. They really are the best!*

2 (5-ounce) cans albacore tuna

2 large stalks celery, diced

2 medium-sized dill pickles, diced

2 tablespoons finely chopped red onion

½ teaspoon freshly ground black pepper

½ cup mayonnaise, to taste

**1**  Drain the tuna and crumble into a medium bowl. Add in the celery, most of the pickles, the onion, and pepper. Add the mayo (just enough to make it as moist as you like!), stir to combine, and taste. If it needs a bit more salt, add more pickles!

**2**  Serve on toasted wheat bread as sandwiches, or top with sliced sharp cheddar cheese and broil until melted and golden!

This tuna salad can be made up to 3 days in advance and stored in the fridge. Stir before serving!

*Serves 3~4*

# slow cooker meaty spaghetti sauce ⟨GF⟩

*You may not think spaghetti sauce is the most exciting thing you have ever seen a recipe for, but let me just tell you, this one is good. There is something about a big pot of tomatoey garlicky goodness that just screams "Yum!"*

*Throw this together in the slow cooker for the day, and dinner is practically served when you get home! (And I'll let you in on a little secret: sometimes I like to eat this delicious sauce by the bowlful and skip the noodles all together. But maybe that's just me?!)*

1½ pounds ground beef

1 large onion, chopped

3 large cloves garlic, minced

½–1 pound fresh mushrooms, quartered

1–2 (26-ounce) jars good marinara sauce (homemade or store-bought)

2 teaspoons dried oregano

1 teaspoon dried rosemary

½ teaspoon crushed red pepper flakes

salt and pepper, to taste

1 parmesan rind*

**1**   In a large skillet, brown the ground beef, remove from the pan (leaving as much grease as possible behind), and place into the bottom of a large (6-quart) slow cooker.

**2**   Dump in the onion, garlic, mushrooms, and the marinara sauce (it's totally up to you if you want a thicker sauce with 1 jar, or a thinner sauce with 2!), and then stir in the spices.

*If you don't already save your parmesan rinds, start right now! When you have used up a chunk, place the rind in a freezer bag and freeze for—well, forever, practically. Just keep adding to the same bag every time you have a new rind. Add it to just about any savory, long-simmering dish, and you will be thrilled with the results!

*Serves 6~8*

# grown-up tuna casserole ⬛GFA

*This is not the tuna casserole you remember eating growing up. This is a crowd-pleasing, grown-up-palate pleasing, every-bit-as-comforting tuna casserole.*

*I worked on this recipe when I lived on my own in the frozen Minnesota tundra. Maybe it was something in the air, but I just couldn't stop with the casseroles. This one was right up on top of my list. And I love it just as much today!*

1 pound short noodles (penne, rotini, etc.)

2 tablespoons butter

½ cup finely chopped onion

½ cup finely chopped fresh mushrooms

3 cups shredded sharp cheddar cheese, divided (2 cups + 1 cup)

2 cans tuna, drained and crumbled

¼ cup finely chopped fresh italian parsley

2 (10.75-ounce) cans condensed cream of mushroom soup (or 3 cups homemade!)

1 cup sour cream

1–2 cups frozen peas, optional (do not thaw!)

**1**  Preheat the oven to 425°F and grease a 9×13" baking dish. Cook the pasta according to package directions. Drain.

**2**  While the pasta is cooking, sauté the onions and mushrooms in butter over medium-high heat until soft and starting to turn golden.

**3**  In a large bowl, gently stir together all of the ingredients except 1 cup of the shredded cheddar cheese. Spread this into the prepared dish, top with the remaining cheese, and bake for 15–20 minutes, until golden and bubbling.

You can make this a day in advance and store in the fridge, covered, before baking. Bake at 350°F for 45–60 minutes until heated through and golden.

If you want to make this tuna casserole well in advance, cool completely (without baking), wrap well with plastic wrap and foil, and freeze. When you are ready to cook it, remove the wrappings and place the casserole on the counter to rest for 30 minutes, while you preheat the oven to 350°F. Bake until golden and bubbling, covering lightly with foil if it is starting to brown too much before it is heated through!

*Makes one 9x13" casserole*

# cookies & bars

93

# the best fudgy from-scratch brownies

*These brownies are my thing. They are my go-to, make any time, I-could-mix-these-in-my-sleep treat. It was the first recipe I made when I got back into the kitchen after having each of my babies, and the one I go back to every time I want to treat someone I love.*

*This really is the only brownie recipe you will ever need. And it's so easy your 10 year old can make them for you (if you have a 10 year old, that is!).*

*They are incredibly easy to throw together, and they also freeze beautifully, making them the BEST make-ahead treat. Any time you feel like turning on your oven, you can have these mixed up in less than 10 minutes and into the oven to bake. Eat a few, freeze the rest, and enjoy having a special treat on hand to spoil the people you love at a moment's notice!*

⅔ cup butter, melted

¾ cup dutch-processed unsweetened cocoa powder

½ teaspoon baking soda

½ cup boiling water

1½ cups sugar

½ cup firmly packed brown sugar

2 teaspoons pure vanilla extract

1 teaspoon salt

2 large eggs

1⅓ cup flour

1½ cup chocolate chips, divided (1 cup + ½ cup)

**1**   Preheat the oven to 350°F. Grease a 9×13" glass baking dish; set aside.

**2**   In a large bowl, whisk together the cocoa powder and baking soda. Whisk in half of the melted butter until smooth, and then whisk in the hot water until smooth and thick.

**3**   Whisk in the sugar, vanilla, salt, and eggs, and then the remaining melted butter, until smooth.

**4**   Sprinkle the flour over the top of the batter in the bowl, and then 1 cup of the chocolate chips on top of that. Use a fork to gently mix in the flour and chocolate chips until just blended.

**5**   Spread the batter into the prepared baking dish, sprinkle evenly with the remaining chocolate chips, and then bake for 35–40 minutes, until just set in the middle and starting to pull away from the sides of the pan. (Always better to underbake than to overbake brownies!)

**6**   Let cool completely before cutting for prettiest results, or dig right in if you can't help yourself!

These brownies freeze beautifully for several weeks! Cool completely, cut into squares, and then wrap well in plastic wrap and foil and place in a freezer bag. Pull them out as you need them—they will thaw quickly on the counter (and taste great still partially frozen too!).

*Serves 20–24*

COOKIES & BARS

# fudgy gluten-free dairy-free brownies ⬛GF

*I like to call these my "Caleb-Brownies," named after a sweet boy in my life who can't have any dairy or gluten. I wanted to make something special for him when his family came over for dinner once, and he was so excited to have something he could enjoy without worrying about it.*

*He still thanks me for them almost every time he sees me (which, by the way, is a great way to get me to bake for you again!), and I have made them many, many times since and always think of Caleb when I do. He brings such a smile to my face!*

*(I have also served these brownies to many unsuspecting non-allergy people without telling them what they are, and no one has guessed yet that they are not regular brownies! I call that a winning recipe!)*

⅔ cup extra-virgin coconut oil, melted

¾ dutch-processed unsweetened cocoa powder

½ teaspoon baking soda

½ cup boiling water

2 cups sugar

2 teaspoons pure vanilla extract

1 teaspoon salt

2 large eggs

1⅓ cups gluten-free all-purpose flour mix*

1½ cups dairy-free chocolate chips

**1**   Preheat the oven to 350°F. Grease a 9×13" glass baking dish with coconut oil; set aside.

**2**   In a large bowl, whisk together the cocoa powder and baking soda. Whisk in half of the melted coconut oil until smooth, and then whisk in the hot water until smooth and thick.

**3**   Whisk in the sugar, vanilla, salt, and eggs, and then the remaining melted coconut oil, until smooth.

*When you measure the flour mix, "fluff" the flour well in the bag before measuring to make sure it's not packed down to firmly! If you have never used any gluten-free flour mixes before, ask around or be open to trying different brands to find one you are happiest with. They are definitely not all created equal!

**4**   Sprinkle the flour over the top of the batter in the bowl, and then 1 cup of the chocolate chips on top of that. Use a fork to gently mix in the flour and chocolate chips until just blended.

**5**   Spread the batter into the prepared baking dish, sprinkle evenly with the remaining chocolate chips, and then bake for 35–40 minutes, until just set in the middle and starting to pull away from the sides of the pan. (Always better to underbake than to over-bake brownies!)

**6**   Let cool completely before cutting for prettiest results, or dig right in if you have some ice cream that needs accompaniment!

These brownies freeze beautifully for up to 3 months! Cool completely, cut into squares, and then wrap well in plastic wrap and foil and place in a freezer bag. Pull them out as you need them—they will thaw quickly on the counter (and taste great still partially frozen too!).

*Serves 20~24*

# butterscotch marshmallow chocolate chip blondies

*The first time I made these bars for my husband, he took one bite and told me, "You should probably stop making brownies now and just make these. You don't need to make anything else!"*

*And I might have to agree with him. If I didn't have to watch my waistline, I would make these all the time! As it is, these are on the rotation for sure. So easy and so good. You'll love them too!*

2½ cups flour

1 teaspoon salt

1 teaspoon baking powder

1 teaspoon cinnamon

1 cup butter, melted and mostly cooled

1¾ cup firmly packed brown sugar

2 large eggs

2 teaspoons pure vanilla extract

1 cup chocolate chips, divided (½ cup + ½ cup)

1 cup butterscotch chips, divided (½ cup + ½ cup)

1 cup mini marshmallows

**1**  Preheat the oven to 350°F. Grease a 9×13" baking dish and set aside. In a medium bowl, whisk together the flour, salt, baking powder, and cinnamon. Set aside.

**2**  In a large mixing bowl, cream together the butter and brown sugar until smooth and fluffy, about 5 minutes. Beat in the eggs and vanilla until well blended.

**3**  Mix in the flour mixture, ½ cup chocolate chips, ½ cup butterscotch chips, and mini marshmallows until combined. Spread the batter into the prepared pan and sprinkle evenly with the remaining chocolate chips and butterscotch chips.

**4**  Bake for 35–40 minutes, until the top is golden brown and the sides are starting to pull away from the edges of the pan. Let cool completely before serving!

These bars freeze great. Let them cool completely, cut, and freeze in a freezer bag or airtight container for up to 3 months. Let thaw on the counter for a few hours or overnight before serving!

*Serves 20–24*

# double coconut chocolate chip cookies

*I am a firm believer of getting the most out of your cookie baking. For me, that means making big batches as often as possible and filling my freezer with whatever I don't need at the moment.*

*Of course, these chewy, delicious cookies can be enjoyed right away, but I dare say they taste even better after they have spent a few nights in the freezer. Give it a try the next time you feel like baking. You'll be glad you did when friends show up unexpected and you have a delicious homemade treat to share with them!*

¾ cup butter, melted and cooled to room temperature

¾ cup virgin coconut oil, melted and cooled to room temperature

2 cups firmly packed brown sugar

1 cup sugar

2 large eggs

2 egg yolks

1 tablespoon pure vanilla extract

4¼ cups all-purpose flour

1½ teaspoons salt

1 teaspoon baking soda

1 cup lightly packed sweetened flaked coconut

2 cups chocolate chips

**1**  In a large mixing bowl, beat together the melted and cooled butter, coconut oil, and sugars until well blended, 3–5 minutes at least.

**2**  Beat in the eggs, egg yolks, and vanilla until blended.

**3**  In a medium bowl, whisk together the flour, salt, and baking soda, and then add that to the dough in the mixer, on low speed, until just blended.

**4**  Stir in the coconut, and chocolate chips and cover the mixing bowl and place it in the fridge to chill for at least 30 minutes.

This is a great pause point—you can leave the cookie dough in the fridge at this point for up to 36 hours! Or you can continue on right away after the 30-minute chill!

**5**  Preheat the oven 325°F. Line several baking sheets with parchment paper.

**6**  Scoop the cookie dough, using a medium-sized scoop, onto the baking sheets, leaving room for the cookies to spread as they bake.

**7**  Bake for 10–12 minutes, until just barely golden brown around the edges. Pull the cookies out of the oven and let cool for 5–10 minutes on the baking sheets before transferring them to a cooling rack to cool completely.

Freeze these cookies in an airtight container or freezer-safe bags for up to 3 months. When you want to serve them, pull them out and let them sit at room temperature for a few minutes or a few hours to soften up again! (Though I like them just as much, if not better, straight out of the freezer!)

*Makes almost 5 dozen three-inch cookies*

# coconut oatmeal sandwich cookies

FOR THE FILLING:

½ cup butter, softened

1 pound (about 4 cups) powdered sugar

2 teaspoons pure vanilla extract

pinch of salt

2–3 tablespoons milk or half & half

*Also known as "The Best Cookies Ever." They really are. The cookie part of the recipe is one of my grandma's most famous cookie recipes. She was often referred to as "The Cookie Lady," so that should give you a hint about her legacy.*

*She baked these Hawaiian oatmeal cookies at least once a week because they were my grandpa's favorite, so we grew up calling them "Grandpa Cookies," and they are a favorite of most of my family and friends!*

*I took this recipe up a notch, turning them into luscious, cream-filled sandwich cookies, but if you want to stay true to Grandma's original, feel free to leave out the filling!*

*My husband took a bite the first time I made them this way and looked at me in a bit of shock and said, "These are the best cookies ever!"—hence the name we use around here.*

*I hope you get a chance to make these and enjoy them as much as we do!*

**1**   Preheat the oven to 375°F. Line several baking sheets with parchment paper and set aside.

**2**   In a large mixing bowl, cream together the butter and sugars until light and fluffy, about 5 minutes. Beat in the eggs and vanilla until smooth.

**3**   Mix in the baking powder, baking soda, and salt quickly, until fully incorporated.

**4**   Mix in the oats and coconut until mixed, and then gently mix in the flour until just combined.

**5**   Using a small (about 1") cookie scoop, scoop the dough onto the parchment-lined baking sheets about 2 inches apart, as these will spread a bit as they bake.

**6**   Flatten each cookie gently with a fork dipped in cold water, to about ¼" thick. Bake for 6–8 minutes, until the cookies are just set and lightly golden brown around the edges. Don't let them get too browned!

**7**   Let the cookies cool on the baking sheets for a few minutes, and then transfer to a cooling rack.

**8**   While the cookies are all cooling, make the cream filling. In a medium mixing bowl, beat together the butter, powdered sugar, vanilla, salt, and 2 tablespoons of the milk until smooth and fluffy. Add a bit more milk as needed until the frosting is still thick, but spreadable. Spread a small amount on the bottom side of half of the cookies and sandwich with another cookie on top.

These cookies freeze wonderfully in an airtight container for up to 2 months!

**FOR THE COOKIES:**

1 cup butter, softened

1 cup sugar

1 cup firmly packed brown sugar

2 large eggs

2 teaspoons pure vanilla extract

2 teaspoons baking powder

1 teaspoon baking soda

1 teaspoon salt

2 cups old-fashioned rolled oats

2 cups lightly packed sweetened-flaked coconut

2¼ cups all-purpose flour

*Makes about 40 sandwich cookies*

# mexican double chocolate sour cream cookies

*I was a little skeptical that these cookies would be the crowd pleaser that they are. Extra chocolatey and moist, of course everyone loves that, but the cinnamon and pinch of cayenne? I just didn't think everyone would love that Mexican flavor combination as much as I do!*

*Fortunately, I was so wrong! Everyone loved these surprising little cookies, and I think you'll see why when you try them!*

3½ cups flour

1 cup dutch-processed unsweetened cocoa powder

2 teaspoons baking powder

1 teaspoon baking soda

1 teaspoon salt

1 teaspoon cinnamon

¼ teaspoon ground cayenne pepper

1 cup butter, softened

1½ cups sugar

1 cup firmly packed brown sugar

2 large eggs

1 cup sour cream

1 tablespoon pure vanilla extract

2 cups semi-sweet chocolate chips

1 cup milk chocolate chips

**1**  In a medium bowl, whisk together the flour, cocoa, baking powder, baking soda, salt, cinnamon, and cayenne until combined.

**2**  In a large mixing bowl, cream together the butter and sugars until very smooth and fluffy, 3–5 minutes. Beat in the eggs, sour cream, and vanilla until smooth.

**3**  Mix in the dry ingredients carefully until just combined, and then stir in the chocolate chips. Cover the dough with plastic wrap and place into the fridge for at least 30 minutes while you preheat the oven.

**4**  Preheat the oven to 350°F. Line a few baking sheets with parchment paper. Scoop the dough onto the parchment with a small scoop and bake for 10–12 minutes, until the cookies are just set. Let them sit a few minutes on the baking sheets before transferring to wire racks to cool completely.

Store cookies in an airtight container in the freezer for up to 3 months! (Or you can scoop all the dough and freeze it on a cookie sheet, then transfer to a freezer-bag for ready to bake cookie dough at any time! Just add a few minutes to the baking time and watch carefully!)

*Makes over 3 dozen cookies*

# molasses crinkles cookies

*There's something about these handwritten recipes from my grandma that just get me every time. I pick up the card and I can almost feel her standing next to me, telling me what to do.*

*These were one of her signature cookies. She made them often and was well known for all of her cookies. She was such a great baker and so loved for her treats; it's pure joy to be able to pass on her traditions to my family and friends!*

1½ cups butter, softened

2 cups firmly packed brown sugar

2 large eggs

½ cup blackstrap molasses

4½ cups flour

2 teaspoons baking soda

2 teaspoons ground ginger

1 teaspoon ground cloves

½ teaspoon salt

extra sugar for sprinkling the cookies

**1**   In a large mixing bowl, cream together the butter and sugar until light and fluffy, 3–5 minutes. Beat in the eggs until smooth, and then beat in the molasses until combined.

**2**   In a medium bowl, whisk together the flour, baking soda, ginger, cloves, and salt, and then carefully stir this dry mixture into the cookie dough until just well combined. Cover the bowl and place it in the fridge to chill for at least 30 minutes.

**3**   Preheat the oven 375°F and line several baking sheets with parchment paper. Scoop out the dough onto the cookie sheets, about 2" apart, and then press down each ball with a fork dipped in cold water. Sprinkle sugar generously over the top of the flattened dough and then bake for 6–8 minutes, until just set.

**4**   Let cool for a few minutes on the baking sheets before transferring to wire racks to cool completely.

Store these cookies in an airtight container in the freezer for up to 3 months!

*Makes over 3 dozen cookies*

# pineapple coconut crumble bars

*These bars are so fun and different. The pineapple filling is tart and sweet, the coconut crust is rich and buttery, and the hint of coconut in the filling is just right!*

*Satisfying your desire to make something different, this is such a fun dessert to make when you want to change things up a bit.*

### FOR THE FILLING:

1 (20-ounce) can crushed pineapple

1 cup sugar

⅓ cup cornstarch

¼ cup orange juice

1 teaspoon salt

2 tablespoons fresh squeezed lemon juice (from one large lemon)

2 tablespoons butter

1 teaspoon coconut extract

### FOR THE CRUST:

2 cups firmly packed brown sugar

2 cups lightly packed sweetened-flaked coconut

2 cups all-purpose flour

2 cups old-fashioned rolled oats

2 teaspoons baking powder

1 teaspoon salt

2 cups butter, softened

**1**  In a medium saucepan, whisk together the pineapple, sugar, cornstarch, orange juice, and salt. Bring to a boil, over medium-high heat, and boil for a few minutes, whisking constantly, until very thick. Remove from the heat and stir in the lemon juice, butter, and coconut extract. Let cool to room temperature before continuing.

**2**  Preheat the oven to 350°F. Grease a 9×13" baking dish, line with parchment, and grease again to make cutting and serving easier.

**3**  In a large mixing bowl, mix together the brown sugar, coconut, flour, oats, baking powder, and salt until combined. Mix in the softened butter until well mixed.

**4**  Press about half of the mixture evenly into the bottom of the prepared baking dish. Spread the cooled pineapple sauce over the top, and then gently crumble the remaining dough over the top of the pineapple. (Use your hands and drop bits of the dough all over the top until it is all used up!) Press down very gently and then bake for 60–70 minutes, until the crust is completely golden and no longer wet.

**5**  Let cool completely, cut, and serve!

Freeze these baked bars, cut and stored in a freezer bag, for up to 3 months.

*Serves 15–20*

# triple batch double peanut butter chocolate chip cookie bars

*These delicious, easy cookie bars are not for the faint of heart. You need a really, really big bowl (6 quarts or bigger!), and you can't be afraid of digging in with your bare hands.*

*But if you ever need to bake for a crowd—or if, like me, you just like to go all out and fill your freezer and your friends' freezers—these are the bars for you.*

*This recipe makes 3 rimmed 11×17" baking sheets almost full of bars. (You can spread the batter thinner to actually fill all 3 pans, but I prefer thick, chewy cookies, so I don't spread them too thin. About ¾" thick, to be exact!)*

*Are you on cookie duty at church? Do you need to take snacks in for your kids' school bake sale or graduation party? Do you want to spoil ALL of your coworkers? Dig in, make this big, huge 12-plus-pound batch of cookie dough, and your day is done.*

*You may not need this recipe every day, but when you do need to bake for a crowd, you will be SO glad you have it!*

8 cups all-purpose flour

1 tablespoon baking powder

1 tablespoon salt

3 cups (1½ pounds) butter, room temperature

2¾ cups creamy peanut butter

2 cups firmly packed brown sugar

2½ cups sugar

6 large eggs

3 egg yolks

2 tablespoons pure vanilla extract

5 cups chocolate chips

3 cups peanut butter chips

**1**   Preheat the oven to 350°F. Line 3 large rimmed baking sheets with parchment. Set aside.

**2**   In a very large (at least 6-quart capacity) bowl, whisk together the flour, baking powder, and salt until combined. Set aside.

**3**   In a large mixing bowl, cream together the butter, peanut butter, and sugars until light and fluffy, 5 minutes at medium-high speed. (If you have a large enough stand mixer, do this in there; otherwise, a hand mixer will work fine!)

**4**   Beat in the eggs, egg yolks, and vanilla until very smooth. Scrape this mixture into the bowl with the flour, dump in the chocolate chips and peanut butter chips, and then mix everything together until combined and no more dry flour remains. (You can use a wooden spoon or, more efficiently, your clean bare hands!)

**5**   Divide the dough evenly onto each of the 3 parchment-lined baking sheets, and then carefully spread the dough out to about ¾" thick or so. It doesn't need to fill the whole pan to the edges, think of it more like a big rectangular cookie!

**6**   Bake each pan for 17–20 minutes, until lightly golden on top and no longer wet looking.

Let cool completely, cut into small bars, and store in airtight freezer containers for up to 6 months!

*Serves 90+*

# butterscotch coconut chocolate chip cookies

*Because sometimes a plain chocolate chip cookie is just not enough. And if you've ever tried this combination of flavors, you will understand.*

*I just can't get enough of these. I love a good simple chocolate chip cookie as much as the next person, but I love these even more!*

1½ cups butter, melted and cooled

2 cups firmly packed brown sugar

1 cup sugar

2 large eggs

2 egg yolks

1 tablespoon pure vanilla extract

4¼ cups flour

1 teaspoon baking soda

1 teaspoon salt

1 cup butterscotch chips

2 cups chocolate chips

2 cups sweetened, flaked coconut

**1**  In a large mixing bowl, cream the butter and sugars until light and fluffy, 3–5 minutes. Beat in the eggs, egg yolks, and vanilla until smooth.

**2**  In a medium bowl, whisk together the flour, baking soda, and salt, and then stir this mixture into the butter mixture until just well combined. Stir in the butterscotch chips, chocolate chips, and coconut.

**3**  Chill the dough for at least 30 minutes or up to 24 hours.

**4**  When you are ready, preheat the oven to 350°F and line several baking sheets with parchment paper. Scoop the dough onto the baking sheets a few inches apart to allow room for the cookies to spread and bake for 10–12 minutes, until just golden around the edges.

**5**  Let cool on the baking sheets, and then transfer to a cooling rack to cool completely.

Freeze these cookies in freezer bags for up to 3 months!

*Makes over 3 dozen cookies*

111

# perfectly moist & chewy oatmeal raisin cookies

*I know, I know. Not everyone loves an oatmeal raisin cookie. But those of us who do love oatmeal raisin cookies REALLY LOVE oatmeal raisin cookies!*

*These are my all-time favorite version of the famous comfort food. Packed full of oats and plump, juicy raisins—and hit with a good dose of spices—these are moist, chewy, and just perfect for an almost-healthy addition to your lunch or a quick on-the-go breakfast!*

1½ cup raisins, soaked*

½ cup flour

1 teaspoon cinnamon

½ teaspoon salt

½ teaspoon baking soda

½ teaspoon cardamom

¼ teaspoon nutmeg

¾ cup butter, melted and cooled

1 cup firmly packed brown sugar

½ cup sugar

1 large egg

1 teaspoon pure vanilla extract

3 cups old-fashioned rolled oats

Place the raisins in a small bowl and add a good splash of pure vanilla extract and 1 teaspoon of cinnamon. Fill with just enough warm water to cover the raisins and let sit for 30–60 minutes. Drain and pat gently on a paper towel.

**1** In a medium bowl, whisk together the flour, cinnamon, salt, soda, cardamom, and nutmeg. Set aside.

**2** In a large mixing bowl, cream together the butter and sugars until light and fluffy, 3–5 minutes. Beat in the egg and vanilla until smooth.

**3** Stir in flour mixture until just combined, and then add in the oats and the soaked (drained) raisins. Cover and place in the fridge to chill for at least 30 minutes.

**4** Preheat the oven to 350°F. Line several baking sheets with parchment, scoop the cookies a few inches apart (they will spread), and bake for 12–18 minutes, depending on size, until just golden around the edges. They will look a little underdone, but they will continue to set up as they cool.

**5** Let them cool completely on the baking sheets, before transferring to airtight containers for storage!

These cookies will keep well in an airtight container at room temperature for up to a week, but even better in the freezer (I freeze all my cookies, even if they will be eaten the next day!). Freeze for up to several weeks!

*Makes over 3 dozen cookies*

# salted caramel frosted dark chocolate brownies ⟨≋GFA⟩

*Sometimes a brownie is just not enough. Sometimes you need salted caramel on top, and this frosting is just about as good as it gets.*

*Yes, homemade brownies are great just as they are, but why not make them extra special every once in a while?*

*And as a bonus, if you are making these for a crowd, the richness of the frosting makes them worth cutting very small and serving many!*

**FOR THE BROWNIES:**

¾ cup dutch-processed unsweetened cocoa powder

½ teaspoon baking soda

⅔ cup melted butter, divided (⅓ cup + ⅓ cup)

½ cup boiling water

1 cup firmly packed brown sugar

1 cup sugar

2 large eggs

½ teaspoon salt

1⅓ cup flour

1 cup chocolate chips

**FOR THE FROSTING:**

1 cup butter

⅓ cup caramel sauce (homemade or store-bought)

1 teaspoon salt

1½–2 cups powdered sugar, to taste

**1**   Preheat the oven to 350°F and grease a 9×13" baking dish. Set aside.

**2**   In a large bowl, whisk together the cocoa powder and baking soda. Whisk in ⅓ cup of the melted butter until smooth, and then whisk in the hot water.

**3**   Whisk in the sugars, salt, and eggs until combined, and then whisk in the remaining ⅓ cup of melted butter until smooth.

**4**   Dump in the flour and chocolate chips together and stir gently with a fork or spatula until just well combined. Spread the batter into the greased baking dish and bake for 35–40 minutes, until just pulling away from the sides and set in the middle.

**5**   While the brownies cool, make the frosting. In a large bowl, beat together the butter, salt, and caramel sauce until smooth. Add in the powdered sugar, ½ cup at a time, until the frosting is just thick and as sweet as you'd like.

**6**   When the brownies are completely cooled, spread the frosting evenly over the top and place in the fridge to set for a while before cutting and serving— for prettiest results.

You can make these brownies, cut them, and freeze them uncovered on a baking sheet until the frosting is firm. Transfer them to an airtight container or freezer bags and freeze for up to 3 months!

*Serves 20–24*

# butterscotch chocolate blondies

*Chocolate blondies? Aren't these just the same as brownies? No, no they're not!*

*Blondies are usually the un-chocolate caramely cousin of a brownie. I added chocolate back into this, but they are still very buttery and caramely and very much blondies.*

*You can use white chocolate chips instead of the butterscotch if you like. Or just substitute more chocolate chips!*

1 cup butter, softened

1¾ cup firmly packed brown sugar

2 teaspoons pure vanilla extract

2 teaspoons ground cinnamon

2 large eggs

2 cups flour

½ cup dutch-processed unsweetened cocoa powder

1 teaspoon baking powder

½ teaspoon salt

¾ cup butterscotch chips, divided (½ cup + ¼ cup)

¾ cup chocolate chips, divided (½ cup + ¼ cup)

**1**   Preheat the oven to 350°F. Grease a 9×13" baking dish. Set aside.

**2**   In a large mixing bowl, cream together the butter and brown sugar until light and fluffy, 3–5 minutes. Beat in the vanilla and cinnamon until blended. Beat in the eggs until well mixed.

**3**   In a small bowl, whisk together the flour, cocoa powder, baking powder, and salt. Stir into the batter, mixing gently until just combined.

**4**   Stir in ½ cup each of the butterscotch and chocolate chips, and then spread into the prepared baking dish. Sprinkle the top with the remaining butterscotch and chocolate chips and bake for 35–45 minutes, until set and starting to pull away from the sides of the pan.

**5**   Cool completely before cutting.

Freeze in an airtight freezer container for up to 3 months!

*Serves 20–24*

COOKIES & BARS

# browned butter cinnamon butterscotch white chocolate chip cookies

*Browned butter makes everything better, am I right?! At least, it does in my world!*

*To make a familiar dessert extra special, brown some butter, let it cool and then use it just like you would regular butter. The toasty, nutty flavor is just perfection!*

1½ cups butter, browned and cooled

2 cups firmly packed brown sugar

1 cup sugar

2 large eggs

2 egg yolks

1 tablespoon pure vanilla extract

4¼ cups all-purpose flour

1½ teaspoons salt

1 teaspoon baking soda

1 teaspoon cinnamon

2 cups cinnamon baking chips*

½ cup butterscotch chips

½ cup white chocolate chips

**1** To brown the butter, melt it over medium heat in a light bottomed skillet. As the butter melts, it will begin to sizzle and foam. Swirl the pan occasionally, until it smells toasty and golden and has browned bits on the bottom. (But watch carefully so it doesn't burn! That's where the light colored pan helps!).

**2** Pour the browned butter into a bowl and set aside to cool to room temperature (you can put it in the fridge to speed this up, if you need!).

**3** In a large mixing bowl, beat together the cooled browned butter and the sugars until well blended, 3–5 minutes.

**4** Beat in the eggs, egg yolks, and vanilla until blended.

**5** In a medium bowl, whisk together the flour, salt, cinnamon, and baking soda, and then add that to the dough in the mixer, on low speed, until just blended.

**6** Stir in the cinnamon, butterscotch and white chocolate chips and then cover the mixing bowl and place it in the fridge to chill for at least 30 minutes.

*Cinnamon chips (cinnamon-flavored chips, like chocolate chips!) are available at some grocery stores. If you can't find any, use extra butterscotch and white chocolate chips and up the ground cinnamon in the recipe to 2 teaspoons!

This is a great pause point—you can leave the cookie dough in the fridge at this point for up to 36 hours! Or you can continue on right away after the 30 minute chill!

**7** Preheat the oven 325°F. Line several baking sheets with parchment paper.

**8** Scoop the cookie dough, using a medium-sized scoop, onto the baking sheets, leaving room for the cookies to spread as they bake.

**9** Bake for 10–12 minutes, until just barely golden brown around the edges. Pull the cookies out of the oven and let cool for 5–10 minutes on the baking sheets before transferring them to a cooling rack to cool completely.

Freeze these cookies in an airtight container or freezer-safe bags for up to 3 months. When you want to serve them, pull them out and let them sit at room temperature for a few minutes or a few hours to soften up again! (Though I like them just as much, if not better, straight out of the freezer!)

*Makes 4~5 dozen cookies*

*Desserts*

# desserts

121

# freezer-friendly salted caramel corn, two ways

**GF**

*I grew up eating this amazing homemade caramel corn every fall and holiday season. My family got the original recipe from our sweet friend Phyllis, and we often refer to this as "Phyllis's Caramel Corn."*

*It was one of the first things I decided I had to make when I moved out on my own, and now it is one of my family's all-time favorite treats. If you don't have an air-popper for your popcorn, it is well worth the $15 investment. You will be so glad you have it! (And you just might use it for all your popcorn needs!)*

*I like to add dark chocolate to half of the batch (because salted caramel and chocolate!), but you definitely don't have to.*

*Or you can add some peanuts and have yourself some homemade cracker jacks!*

¾ cup popcorn kernels (popped—about 6 quarts)

1 cup butter

2 cups firmly packed brown sugar

½ cup corn syrup

2 teaspoons salt

½ teaspoon ground cinnamon

½ teaspoon baking soda

2 teaspoons pure vanilla extract

1 cup chopped dark chocolate, optional

**1** Pop the popcorn using your air-popper (or whatever no-oil method you like—even plain microwave popcorn can be used) and transfer to a very large bowl, trying not to get too many unpopped kernels in. Set aside.

**2** Preheat the oven to 250°F. Grease two rimmed baking sheets. Set aside.

**3** In a medium saucepan, melt the butter over medium-high heat and stir in the brown sugar, corn syrup, salt, and cinnamon. Stir constantly until just boiling, and then boil without stirring for 5 minutes, until very golden and fragrant.

**4** Remove from the heat and stir in the baking soda and vanilla (careful, this will foam up!) until light and smooth, and then pour the hot caramel over the popcorn, stirring well until completely coated (this is easier with a helper!).

**5** Spread the caramel corn evenly onto the two rimmed baking sheets and bake for 30 minutes, rotating the pans and stirring gently halfway through.

**6** Remove from the oven and sprinkle the chopped chocolate over one of the pans, stirring gently to incorporate. (You just want melted bits, so don't stir too much!)

**7** Cool the caramel corn completely before breaking up and placing in airtight containers (these will store at room temperature for up to 1 week!).

Caramel corn freezes great for up to 3 months! Cool completely, fill into freezer-bags, and freeze. No need to thaw!

*Makes about 5 quarts*

# pumpkin pecan crumble (GFA)

*If you love pumpkin pie but don't love pie crust—or you just don't have time to make your own—this is the pumpkin dessert for you!*

*Everything you love about pumpkin pie, but even better, with a buttery crumbly topping and no crust. This dessert whips up so quickly, you will never need to buy a pre-made pumpkin pie again!*

*Serve with lots of fresh whipped cream, of course, and if you decide to eat this for breakfast, I promise I won't judge!*

### FOR THE FILLING:

4 large eggs

1 large (29-ounce) can pumpkin purée

1½ cups sugar

1 tablespoon pumpkin pie spice

1 teaspoon ground cinnamon

2 (12-ounce) cans evaporated milk

### FOR THE TOPPING:

¾ cup flour (gluten-free flour blend, if needed)

1 cup firmly packed brown sugar

½ teaspoon salt

2 teaspoons pumpkin pie spice

1 cup old-fashioned rolled oats

½ cup butter, melted

**1**   Preheat the oven to 425°F. Grease a 9×13" baking dish. Set aside.

**2**   In a large bowl, beat the eggs until blended. Whisk in the pumpkin, sugar, and spices until smooth. Pour in the evaporated milk and stir gently until combined. Pour this filling into the greased pan and bake for 15 minutes.

**3**   While the filling is baking, stir together the topping ingredients until moistened and well combined.

**4**   When the 15 minutes is up, lower the temperature to 350°F, open the oven, and sprinkle the crumble topping evenly over the hot filling in the pan. Close the door and bake for 60–70 minutes, until a toothpick inserted near the center comes out clean and the topping is golden.

**5**   Let cool to room temperature, and then place in the fridge to chill for a few hours or overnight. Serve with lots of fresh whipped cream and, of course, some hot coffee to wash it down!

*Serves 10–12*

# roasted strawberry–rhubarb sauce ⬛GF

*I have always loved classic—simmer-on-the-stove-with-a-bit-of-thickener—rhubarb sauce. Actually, I'm pretty sure I have eaten my own weight's worth over my lifetime.*

*But this simple roasted sauce has won me over. I don't think I will ever go back to simmering on the stove!*

*The color is out of this world. The smell when you open the oven door will blow your mind. If you like rhubarb and strawberries at all, this almost hands-free treat will make your day!*

6 cups halved or quartered strawberries, depending on size

6 cups diced rhubarb (about ½" chunks)

⅔ cup sugar

**1** Preheat the oven to 450°F. Line two large rimmed-baking sheets with a generous sheet of parchment (overhanging, to catch all the juicy syrup!).

**2** In a large bowl, gently toss the strawberries and rhubarb with the sugar, to coat. Dump half of the mixture onto each baking sheet, spreading out into an even layer.

**3** Roast for 20–25 minutes, until the rhubarb is tender and the strawberries have released lots of their syrupy juice. Let cool just until you can handle the pans, and then transfer the mixture to a large bowl (if you're careful, you can just pick up the parchment and slowly pour it all into the bowl!). Let cool completely, and then cover and chill in the fridge for up to 5 days!

**4** Serve over good vanilla ice cream for dessert, or you can take this into the breakfast realm with a bowl of plain greek yogurt, some sauce, and good granola!

*Serves 4~6*

# browned butter frosting  ⌐GF

*Yes, this frosting recipe needed its own spot. It's just too good to stick to one recipe. You can spread this on your favorite soft cookie (pumpkin? gingerbread?), on top of cinnamon rolls, or even on a simple cake.*

*You can even just make a batch and eat it by the spoonful. I may have done that a few times!*

1 cup butter

¼ cup heavy cream

½ teaspoon pure vanilla extract

4 cups whisked powdered sugar*

**1**    To brown the butter, melt it over medium heat in a light bottomed skillet. As the butter melts, it will begin to sizzle and foam. Let it go, swirling the pan occasionally, until it smells toasty and golden and has browned bits on the bottom. (Watch carefully so it doesn't burn! That's where the light colored pan helps!)

**2**    Pour the browned butter into a large mixing bowl and set aside to cool to room temperature (you can put it in the fridge to speed this up, if you need!). When cool, beat with the heavy cream, vanilla, and the powdered sugar until smooth and as thick as you would like.

*It is so hard to get an accurate measurement with powdered sugar. I measure by "fluffing" the sugar well with a whisk before measuring, but just use what you need. Start with 2 cups and add a ½ cup at a time until it is as sweet as you'd like!

This frosting will keep well, covered tightly, in the fridge for up to 1 week . . . if you don't eat it all before then!

*Serves 12~18*

127

# pumpkin cupcakes with cinnamon cream cheese frosting

**GF**

*Pumpkin everything. That's my motto every fall. Maybe you understand that feeling?*

*I could probably survive on a pumpkin-everything diet. Pumpkin slow cooker oatmeal, pumpkin chili, pumpkin cupcakes . . . Yep. I could do it.*

*These cupcakes are moist, flavorful, and perfect for a simple fall dessert that is sure to please everyone. And you really can't go wrong with the frosting.*

*Cinnamon + cream cheese + pumpkin is just about the best combo there is!*

**FOR THE CUPCAKES:**

1½ cups flour

1 cup firmly packed brown sugar

1 teaspoon baking powder

1 teaspoon baking soda

1 teaspoon salt

1 tablespoon pumpkin pie spice

1 teaspoon cinnamon

¾ cup butter, melted and cooled

4 large eggs

2 cups pumpkin purée

1 teaspoon pure vanilla extract

**FOR THE FROSTING:**

½ cup butter, softened

1 (8-ounce) package cream cheese, softened

1½–2 cups powdered sugar*

1 teaspoon pure vanilla extract

2 teaspoons cinnamon

**1**  Preheat the oven to 350°F. Line 2 mini-muffin pans with paper liners.

**2**  In a large bowl, whisk together the flour, brown sugar, baking powder, baking soda, salt, pumpkin pie spice, and cinnamon until combined.

**3**  In another bowl, whisk together the melted and cooled butter, eggs, pumpkin, and vanilla until smooth. Pour the wet ingredients into the dry ingredients and whisk until just combined.

**4**  Scoop the batter into the muffin liners, about ¾ full, and bake for 12–15 minutes, or until the tops spring back when gently pressed. (You may or may not use all the liners. It depends on your pans and how full you fill each one. Don't worry if you don't—just take out the empty liners and save for another time!). You can also bake these in regular muffin tins . . . adjust time to about 20 minutes and watch carefully!

**5**  **TO MAKE THE FROSTING:** In a large mixing bowl, cream together the cream cheese, butter, vanilla, and cinnamon until smooth. Add in 1½ cups of powdered sugar and mix until smooth. Taste and add more powdered sugar if needed! (*Powdered sugar can be so hard to measure. Don't worry if you need much less or much more. Just keep adding until the frosting is thick and sweet enough for your liking!)

**6**  When the cupcakes are done, let them cool completely, and then frost. Sprinkle the tops with a bit more cinnamon for decoration, and serve!

The cupcakes and frosting can be made in advance. Let the cupcakes cool completely, and then freeze for up to 1 month. Thaw overnight on the counter. The frosting can be made a week in advance, covered, and kept in the fridge. Let it soften for several hours at room temperature before frosting!

You can also make the cupcakes completely (frosted and everything) and store in the fridge for up to 24 hours. Let warm up a bit at room temperature before serving!

If you like a LOT of frosting, or plan on making cinnamon rolls sometime the same week, make a double batch of the frosting and store in the fridge!

*Serves 18–24*

# rhubarb custard cake, from scratch ⟍GFA

*Why the clarification that this simple dessert is made from scratch? Well, if you are a Midwest native, you are likely familiar with the much-loved Rhubarb Custard Cake. You take a cake mix, mix it according to the package, put rhubarb, sugar, and cream on top, and bake it.*

*Keeping true to the flavor, I wanted to get rid of that boxed cake mix. I just don't care for them. There may seem like a few steps to this cake, but I promise it is easy and so worth it. Give it a try next time you get your hands on some fresh rhubarb!*

*This not-too-sweet cake forms a beautiful, rich rhubarb custard on the bottom as it bakes. In my world, it totally passes as a breakfast cake.*

*(But I live in a world where cake for breakfast is totally normal. I'm just saying!)*

1 cup flour

1½ teaspoons baking powder

¼ teaspoon salt

5 eggs, separated

¾ cup sugar

⅓ cup milk

1 teaspoon pure vanilla extract

¼ cup sugar

4 cups chopped rhubarb

¾ cup sugar

2 cups heavy cream

**1**   Preheat the oven to 350°F. Grease a 9×13" baking dish. Set aside. In a small bowl, whisk together the flour, baking powder, and salt. Set aside.

**2**   Separate the egg yolks from the whites into two separate bowls. Set aside.

**3**   In a large bowl, beat together the egg yolks and ¾ cup sugar until very pale yellow in color. Stir in the milk and vanilla until combined. Gently whisk the flour mixture into the beaten egg yolks mixture until combined.

**4**   In a separate large, very clean mixing bowl (egg whites won't whip well if there is any grease at all in the bowl or on the beaters!), with the wire whisk attachment, beat the egg whites until foamy and soft.

**5**   Slowly pour in ¼ cup sugar while the mixer is beating and continue to beat until stiff, glossy peaks form (pull the whisk out and a stiff little peak should be left, not a soft, slumpy mountain). Don't let the whites beat to a dry texture again, or you will need to use new whites!

**6**   Gently fold the beaten eggs whites into the batter, a few scoops at a time, until the mixture is light and fluffy and all the whites are incorporated. Spread this batter evenly into the greased baking dish.

**7**   Gently scatter the chopped rhubarb all over the top of the batter, and then sprinkle evenly with ¾ cup sugar and drizzle all over with the heavy cream.

**8**   Bake for 40–50 minutes, until the top is golden and the cake is set (springs back when pressed gently on the top). Let cool completely in the pan and serve at room temperature, or even cold . . . with whipped cream or ice cream if you want to make it fancy.

This cake can be served the day it's made, but it tastes even better cold the next day, so make this the night before you want it, cover it well, and place in the fridge! So good!

*Serves 8–10*

# smooth old-fashioned fudge 🌿GF

*I got this recipe from an old family friend. It has been a favorite of my dad's for years and he has always called it "Kay's Fudge."*

*Whatever you call it, this fudge is delicious. It is smooth, creamy, rich, and easy to make. No cheater ingredients, and no candy thermometers needed. If I can make this, you can too!*

*Add in whatever you'd like—nuts, marshmallows, peppermint—once you learn the base, you can make it however you'd like!*

4½ cups sugar

1 (12-ounce) can evaporated milk

1 (1-ounce) square bittersweet chocolate, chopped

3 cups semi-sweet chocolate chips

1 teaspoon pure vanilla extract

1 cup butter, softened

1 cup chopped nuts or mini marshmallows, optional*

**1**  Butter a 9" square baking dish, line it with parchment, and butter again. Set aside. In a large bowl, place the chopped chocolate, chocolate chips, vanilla, and butter. Set aside.

**2**  In a medium pot, stir together the sugar and evaporated milk. Bring to a boil over medium-high heat, stirring constantly, and then boil without stirring for 9 minutes.

If your pan is not very heavy bottomed, it may get a little too brown on the bottom. Don't worry! Just don't scrape the pan when you pour out the hot mixture! Any burnt bits will stay there, and you can soak them off later!

**3**  Pour the hot milk mixture over the chocolate in the bowl and let sit for 1 or 2 minutes, and then stir until the fudge comes together and is smooth and thick. (Keep stirring if it seems like it's not coming together . . . don't give up!)

*If you are adding anything in, now is the time.

**4**  Pour the fudge into the buttered dish and place in the fridge to cool completely and set.

**5**  Pull the pan out, cut the fudge into bite-sized cubes and place into an airtight container.

This fudge will last for up to 2 weeks in the fridge, if you don't eat it all before that! Let sit at room temperature for about 30 minutes before serving for best flavor and texture.

*Serves 36~40*

# almond poppyseed ice cream ⟨GF⟩

*Ice cream for breakfast?! Why didn't I think of this? Oh, wait.*

*This was not my flavor combo idea. But how could I resist? And yes, it really does taste like you should be eating it for breakfast, which makes my ice cream–loving heart incredibly happy!*

2 cups heavy cream

1 cup low fat milk

2 teaspoons pure almond extract

2 large organic eggs*

¾ cup sugar

2 tablespoons poppy seeds

pinch of salt

**1**  In a medium bowl, stir together the cream, milk, and almond extract.

**2**  In a large bowl, beat the eggs until light, 2–3 minutes. Slowly pour in the sugar, while the mixer is on low, and continue to beat until very light and fluffy. Stir in the cream/milk mixture and the salt and poppy seeds and pour into the bowl of your ice cream maker, according to the manufacturer's directions.

**3**  When the ice cream is set (like soft serve), transfer the to a freezer-safe container and place in the freezer for at least 3 hours or up to 1 week!

*There are raw eggs in this ice cream. That has never stopped me from loving and enjoying this, nor has it ever made my family or friends sick. I use only fresh, organic eggs for this. If you are concerned, you can find pasteurized raw eggs at some grocery stores!

*Serves 4~6*

# brown sugar cinnamon ice cream 🌿GF

*I have had friends call this "snickerdoodle ice cream," and that is definitely a fitting name, but I can't help but go back to thinking of this as "cereal milk ice cream" because, to me, it tastes just like the milk left over after you eat a bowl of cinnamon toast cereal!*

*Whatever you call this, you will love it. It's different and special and just lovely!*

2 cups heavy cream

1 cup low fat milk

1 teaspoon pure vanilla extract

2 large organic eggs*

¾ cup firmly packed brown sugar

2 teaspoons cinnamon

pinch of salt

**1**   In a medium bowl, stir together the cream, milk, and almond extract.

**2**   In a large bowl, beat the eggs until light, 2–3 minutes. Slowly pour in the sugar, while the mixer is on low, and continue to beat until very light and fluffy. Stir in the cream/milk mixture and the salt and cinnamon and pour into the bowl of your ice cream maker, according to the manufacturer's directions.

**3**   When the ice cream is set (like soft serve), transfer the to a freezer-safe container and place in the freezer for at least 3 hours or up to 1 week!

*There are raw eggs in this ice cream. That has never stopped me from loving and enjoying this, nor has it ever made my family or friends sick. I use only fresh, organic eggs for this. If you are concerned, you can find pasteurized raw eggs at some grocery stores!

*Serves 4~6*

THE MAKE-AHEAD KITCHEN | ANNALISE THOMAS

# dark chocolate cardamom orange ice cream

**GF**

*If I had to pick only one ice cream to eat ever again in my life, this one would be it.*

*I know that's a tall order, but I just can't even describe how happy this ice cream makes me. Without compare, this is the best ice cream I have ever put in my mouth. And that's saying a lot.*

*If you like it even a fraction of how much I do, you will be pleasantly surprised by the flavor combo! I really wish I could make this for you all so you could understand the feelings it gives me. But since I can't, all I can do is ask that you give this a try!*

*(If you think you won't like the texture of the orange zest in the finished ice cream, strain it out of the milk mixture after letting it sit for at least 30 minutes in the fridge! The bits don't bother me at all!)*

2 cups heavy cream

1 cup low fat milk

¼ cup dutch-processed unsweetened cocoa powder

1 teaspoon pure vanilla extract

1 teaspoon ground cardamom

finely grated zest of one large orange

2 large organic eggs*

¾ cup sugar

pinch of salt

**1**   In a medium bowl, stir together the cream, milk, cocoa powder, vanilla, cardamom, and orange zest.

**2**   In a large bowl, beat the eggs until light, 2–3 minutes. Slowly pour in the sugar, while the mixer is on low, and continue to beat until very light and fluffy. Stir in the cream/milk mixture and the salt and pour into the bowl of your ice cream maker, according to the manufacturer's directions.

**3**   When the ice cream is set (like soft serve), transfer the to a freezer-safe container and place in the freezer for at least 3 hours or up to 1 week!

*There are raw eggs in this ice cream. That has never stopped me from loving and enjoying this, nor has it ever made my family or friends sick. I use only fresh, organic eggs for this. If you are concerned, you can find pasteurized raw eggs at some grocery stores!

*Serves 4~6*

137

# fudge truffle cheesecake  GFA

*Cheesecake is one of the easiest make-ahead desserts there is. It is so fun and special, and yes, it has a few steps, but you can make it any time you feel like it and place it in the freezer for a special day in the future!*

*Or, like us, you can make it, eat a few slices, and wrap up the leftovers in a few large wedges so that you can pull out just a bit of dessert when you're craving it!*

*This rich, incredibly chocolatey cheesecake is the perfect dessert for the chocolate lover in your life. It really doesn't get much better than this!*

*Also, if you are making a gluten-free version, just use gluten-free sandwich cookies for the crust and you're all set!*

**FOR THE CRUST:**

20 regular chocolate sandwich cookies

4–5 tablespoons melted butter

**FOR THE FILLING:**

2½ (8-ounce) packages of cream cheese (20 ounces total), softened

1 cup sugar

¼ cup dutch-processed unsweetened cocoa powder

1 cup sour cream

3 large eggs

1 egg yolk

1 teaspoon pure vanilla extract

¼ teaspoon salt

2 cups chocolate chips, melted and slightly cooled*

½ cup hot fudge sauce

**1** *Place the chocolate chips in a medium bowl and melt in the microwave, stirring well every 30 seconds, until just fully melted. Set aside to cool down a bit before using later.

**2** Preheat the oven to 350°F. Crush the chocolate sandwich cookies into fine crumbs and stir in enough melted butter to just moisten completely (grab a small handful and squeeze . . . it should mostly stick together!). Press into the bottom and partway up the sides of a 9–10" springform pan. Bake for 10–15 minutes, until the crust is just set (not longer looks wet). Cool completely on a wire rack while you prepare the filling.

**3** Preheat the oven to 325°F, wrap the outside of the springform pan well with two layers of foil, and place in a large roasting pan. Set a pot of water to boil (you will use this for a water bath for the cheesecake).

**4** In a large mixing bowl or a large food processor, mix the cream cheese, sugar, and cocoa together until smooth. Mix in the sour cream until well combined. Add the eggs and egg yolk, one at a time, until smooth, and then mix in the vanilla and salt.

**5** Mix in the melted chocolate chip mixture until smooth, and then pour the batter into the cooled crust in the springform pan.

**6** Tap the pan on the counter a few times to get out any air bubbles and smooth the top. Dollop the hot fudge sauce (not actually heated!) by small spoonfuls all over the top of the batter. Gently swirl all through the top with a knife, and then place the pan into the roasting pan and into the oven.

**7** Once you have set the pan into the oven, pour the boiling water into the roasting pan (being careful not to splash into the cheesecake!) up to about halfway up the sides of the springform pan.

**8** Bake for 60–70 minutes (start checking at 50 minutes, depending on the size of your pan!) until the cheesecake is almost set (still jiggly in the center). Turn off the oven, crack the door open, and then let the cheesecake cool in the oven until the oven is completely cooled off.

**9** Remove the cheesecake from the water bath, carefully removing the foil and drying on a towel, and then place on a cooling rack to cool completely. As it cools down and starts to settle, carefully run a thin, sharp knife around the edges of the pan to loosen the cheesecake so it doesn't crack.

**10** If it DOES crack, don't worry! Top with more fudge sauce and no one will know! Or just cut and serve with lots of whipped cream! Yum!

Like all cheesecakes, this one freezes beautifully. Let cool completely and place in the fridge to chill overnight. When it is very firm, wrap well in plastic wrap and foil and place in the freezer for up to 3 months!

Thaw on the counter for an hour or so before serving!

*Serves 12–16*

# coconut tres leches sheet cake

*Tres leches is traditionally made with evaporated milk, condensed milk, and heavy cream. I love the original as much as the next person, but I just couldn't help thinking about how good this would taste with a bunch of coconut thrown in the mix, and boy was I right!*

*If you love coconut and extra-moist cakes, this is right up your alley. And the fact that it tastes best after a day or two in the fridge makes this just about the best dessert to make for a crowd!*

1 cup flour

1½ teaspoons baking powder

¼ teaspoon salt

5 large eggs, yolks and whites separated

1 cup sugar, divided (¾ cup + ¼ cup)

1 teaspoon pure vanilla extract

⅓ cup coconut milk (or regular milk)

1 (14-ounce) can coconut milk, well stirred

1 (14-ounce) can sweetened condensed milk

1¼ cups heavy cream, divided (¼ cup + 1 cup)

1½ cups flaked coconut, plain or toasted

**1** Preheat the oven to 350°F. Grease a 9×13" baking dish. Set aside. In a small bowl, whisk together the flour, baking powder, and salt. Set aside.

**2** Separate the egg yolks from the whites into two separate bowls. Set aside.

**3** In a large bowl, beat together the egg yolks and ¾ cup sugar until very pale yellow in color. Stir in the ⅓ cup milk and vanilla until combined. Gently whisk the flour mixture into the beaten egg yolks mixture until combined.

**4** In a separate large, clean mixing bowl (egg whites won't whip well if there is any grease at all in the bowl or on the beaters!) with the wire whisk attachment, beat the egg whites until foamy and soft.

**5** Slowly pour in ¼ cup sugar while the mixer is beating and continue to beat until stiff, glossy peaks form (pull the whisk out and a stiff little peak should be left, not a soft, slumpy mountain). *Don't let the whites beat to a dry texture again, or you will need to use new whites!*

**6** Gently fold the beaten eggs whites into the batter, a few scoops at a time, until the mixture is light and fluffy and all the whites are incorporated. Spread this batter evenly into the greased baking dish.

**7** Bake for 35–45 minutes, until the cake is golden and springs back when gently pressed down on the center.

**8** Remove the cake to a cooling rack and let cool completely. When the cake is cool, pour the coconut milk, sweetened condensed milk, and ¼ cup of the heavy cream evenly over the top. Cover and place in the fridge to soak in all the goodness overnight.

**9** To toast the coconut, spread the flaked coconut onto a baking sheet and place in a preheated 350°F for about 10 minutes, until golden. Watch carefully so it doesn't burn! Let cool completely, and then store in an airtight container until you are ready to serve!

**10** When you are ready to serve the cake, whip the remaining cream and spread over the top of the cake. Then sprinkle the top with the coconut and serve!

*Serves 12–15*

Drinks

# drinks

# not-so-green smoothies  ⟨GF⟩

*We all know we are supposed to be eating about as many leafy greens as we can stomach, right? I don't know about you, but no matter how good they are, I just can't eat salads all day, every day. And even if I could, my kids definitely wouldn't!*

*So, this is how I sneak lots of greens into our diets. Packed into smoothies, hidden with dark frozen berries (blueberries, blackberries), and sweetened with a banana and some coconut milk.*

*You will love getting in your greens with these delicious, healthy smoothies!*

1 ripe banana

2 big handfuls (or more) dark leafy greens (spinach, mixed greens, etc.)

1½ cups frozen mixed berries

1 teaspoon cinnamon

pinch of salt

up to 1 cup coconut milk or juice, to taste

**1**  Place the banana in the bottom of your blender and pack in the greens and frozen berries, the cinnamon, and salt. Add in as much coconut milk or juice as you'd like to get the texture you prefer. Start with less and add more if it's too thick. This will vary depending on the strength and size of your blender!

**2**  Enjoy immediately, or freeze individual portions for future drinks!

These smoothies can be frozen for quick, on-the-go healthy snacks! Pour into freezer-safe containers or freezer bags and freeze for up to 3 months. Thaw in the fridge overnight, or in your lunch box all morning, and transfer to a cup! Enjoy!

*Serves 3–4*

# hot cranberry pineapple punch

**◇GF**

*My aunt Judi has a wonderful recipe for "percolator punch" that I have always been thrilled with. For so many years, I avoided making it because I have never owned a percolator.*

*One day, I smacked myself in the face when I realized my slow cooker would work just as well. Goodness, I had been missing out!*

*This is my favorite hot fall and winter party punch. Everyone loves it and it makes the house smell amazing. It's a win-win!*

3 cups cranberry juice

3 cups pineapple juice

1½ cups water

¼ cup firmly packed brown sugar

1½ teaspoons whole cloves

2 large cinnamon sticks

pinch of salt

1 cup fresh (or frozen) unsweetened cranberries

**1**  In a medium pot, stir together all of the ingredients and heat over medium-low heat until it is hot. Reduce heat to very low and simmer for as long as you'd like (it will taste even better as it sits), or at least until the cranberries start to burst and the punch is nice and hot!

This hot punch can easily be mixed up in a pitcher in the fridge for up to a week before heating, or can even be heated in the slow cooker all day for a hands-off treat. Serve hot!

*Serves 12–15*

# slow cooker chai spiced cider  GF

*I know hot spiced cider might not seem like the most exciting thing to find in a cookbook, but let me tell you . . . This stuff is amazing!*

*So warm and cozy and a nice kick of spice and caffeine (you can use decaf chai if you want!), you may never go back to the plain old stuff after trying this chai cider!*

4 cups (one 32-ounce container) Tazo chai concentrate

8 cups good apple juice

4 large cinnamon sticks, broken in half

2 teaspoons whole cloves

1 teaspoon whole peppercorns

10 whole cardamom pods, lightly crushed

pinch of salt

**1** In a large slow cooker, stir together all of the ingredients, and then heat on LOW for several hours until nice and hot!

This spiced cider can be reheated several times. Make a full batch on a cold day ,and if it doesn't get finished off, just store it in the fridge and reheat it the next day!

*Serves 10~12*

# index

## About the Author

Annalise is a big-city girl married to a small-town boy. Every day is a joy and a challenge as she learns to live and love this small-town life. Annalise is a foodie with a deep passion for everything edible and for sharing what she loves with others. Annalise is a wife and mom, a baker, a cook, and a blogger. She and her family live a very real life and eat as much real food as possible.

SCAN to visit

WWW.SWEETANNAS.COM